VOCABULARY QUIZ WORKBOOK

—With Answer Key—

VOCABULARY QUIZ WORKBOOK

—With Answer Key—

By

Marie Ignatz

Edited by

Mary Frances Lester

Based on 6 Books by Mary Fabyan Windeatt:

The Children of Fatima

The Curé of Ars

The Little Flower

Patron Saint of First Communicants

The Miraculous Medal

St. Louis De Montfort

TAN BOOKS AND PUBLISHERS, INC.

Rockford, Illinois 61105

TAN BOOKS AND PUBLISHERS, INC.
P.O. Box 424
Rockford, Illinois 61105
2003

A Word To Those Who Use This Book

Welcome to this *Vocabulary Quiz Workbook*. We trust that using this workbook will be both an educational experience and an enjoyable experience.

The main instruction to be given for this workbook is the following:

Remember that this is a **vocabulary** workbook, not a book of questions about the events in the stories. For each "question," remember that you are being asked about the meaning of the **word**, not about the meaning of the story. Very often, even the incorrect answers will make good sense if "plugged in" to the story in place of the vocabulary word, but only one of the answers will mean the same thing as **the vocabulary word**. That one answer is the correct answer.

There are 2,020 "questions" in this workbook, with a few words being repeated, since a word may appear in more than one of the six Windeatt books from which the words were taken. But this is all for the good, as repetition is one of the main tools of learning.

All in all, this *Vocabulary Quiz Workbook* should help you to learn new words, to learn new uses of words you already know, and to sharpen your understanding of the meaning of words with which you are *somewhat* familiar. Reading is the easiest and most enjoyable way to build one's vocabulary, and this book will help you get the most out of your reading without bogging you down with writing out definitions. Plus, this book will teach the meaning of many Catholic terms—such as *novice, beatification, mortification, canon, cloistered, Matins, catacombs*—thus helping you to be comfortable with the reading of other Catholic books.

There will be more than one way to use this book. It can be used before, during or after reading the chapter from which the words were taken. You will find that the words in the workbook appear in the same sequence as they appear in the Windeatt book from which they were taken. In most cases there will be no problem with using this workbook even *without* reading the chapter, though occasionally the answer choices may seem odd unless one sees how the vocabulary word was used in the sentence.

We have conceived this workbook not primarily as a dictionary exercise but primarily as an exercise in using one's head. Using the dictionary can be a back-up system, if desired, although the correct answers may not be found verbatim in the dictionary—just as the answers to the vocabulary portion of the SAT (or other standardized tests) may not be found verbatim in the dictionary. There will be great profit in simply making well thought-out guesses as to the correct answers, then checking one's answers against the Answer Key. Whenever you find that you have chosen an incorrect answer, just make a mental note of the correct answer and consider this a learning experience. In that way, the use of this workbook will be not drudgery but fun, resulting in a painless expansion and fine-tuning of your vocabulary.

CONTENTS

Vocabulary Quizzes

Lists of Vocabulary Words

Answer Key

VOCABULARY QUIZZES

Instructions: Circle the letter of the answer which best matches the meaning of the vocabulary word.

The Angel
of Peace

Chapter 1

Perfect Score: 100　　　　　　　　　　　**Score:** _____

1. natives
  a) people who have lived in a particular place for a few years
  b) people who are visiting the place where they were born
  c) people who have just moved to a particular place
  d) people who were born in a particular place

2. arisen
  a) gotten up from bed
  b) appeared in the doorway
  c) awakened from slumber
  d) arrived somewhere

3. dreary
  a) dreaded
  b) gloomy
  c) dreadful
  d) flat

4. surmounted by
  a) with something near it
  b) with something below it
  c) with something beside it
  d) with something on top of it

5. inclined to
  a) having an opinion about
  b) having a tendency toward
  c) having confidence in
  d) in the habit of

6. expanse
  a) a large field
  b) a large, uninterrupted space
  c) a large, crowded space
  d) a spacious room

7. awestruck
  a) filled with shock and dismay
  b) filled with eagerness and longing
  c) filled with joy and gratitude
  d) filled with reverence and wonder

8. merciful
  a) lofty, sublime
  b) compassionate, charitable
  c) prayerful, meditative
  d) meek, humble

9. sacrifice
  a) something offered to God
  b) something commanded by God
  c) something taught by God
  d) a sacramental

10. reparation
  a) sorrow for sin
  b) making up for sin
  c) asking for forgiveness
  d) asking for mercy

11. petition
  a) demand
  b) request
  c) suggestion
  d) repentance

12. submission
  a) courage, fortitude
  b) honor and glory
  c) obedience, acceptance
  d) free will

13. suspended
  a) moved
  b) ornamented
  c) held up
  d) created

14. prostrated oneself
  a) lay facedown
  b) bowed one's head
  c) knelt
  d) bowed from the waist

15. profoundly
  a) deeply, intensely
  b) faithfully, obediently
  c) religiously, spiritually
  d) compassionately, kindly

16. outrages
  a) dishonest words
  b) noisy behaviors
  c) terrible offenses
  d) constant annoyances

17. sacrilege
  a) refusal to believe in Catholic teaching
  b) act of disobedience toward lawful authority
  c) abuse of a holy person or thing
  d) any scandalous behavior

18. indifference
  a) difference of opinion
  b) angry argument
  c) lack of interest
  d) similarity of opinion

19. sublime
  a) exalted, lofty
  b) powerful, mighty
  c) reverent, humble
  d) happy, joyful

20. beckoned
  a) gestured for someone to back off
  b) gestured for someone to step aside
  c) gestured for someone to obey
  d) gestured for someone to come

Another Visitor	**Chapter 2**	Text Pages 10-17

Perfect Score: 100   Score: _____

1. converted
  a) punished for sin
  b) freed from suffering
  c) changed in way of life
  d) persuaded to visit a priest

2. pasturing
  a) taking to a grazing area
  b) feeding in a barn
  c) putting into a confined area
  d) taking care of

3. hollow
  a) rocky, hilly area
  b) wide open space
  c) enclosed empty space
  d) mountainous region

4. doubtfully
  a) with uncertainty
  b) with worry
  c) without worry
  d) thoughtfully

5. shimmering
a) puffy
b) shaking, quaking
c) transparent
d) glimmering, shining

6. mantle
a) long, loose gown
b) cloak
c) nun's habit
d) long coat

7. burnished
a) polished
b) ornamented
c) expensive
d) beautiful

8. exquisite
a) very expressive
b) very fragile
c) of special sentimental value
d) of great, delicate beauty

9. ventured
a) hesitated to proceed
b) dared to proceed
c) proceeded with assistance
d) proceeded without assistance

10. hesitantly
a) reluctantly
b) in a soft voice
c) humbly
d) helpfully

11. astonished
a) terrified
b) amazed
c) overjoyed
d) angry

12. apparition
a) meditation
b) vision
c) mysterious idea
d) superstition

13. glorious
a) exciting
b) happy
c) memorable
d) magnificent

14. alarm
a) surprise
b) vague uneasiness
c) sudden fear
d) eagerness

15. have strayed
a) have wandered away
b) have walked around
c) have run away
d) have hidden

16. forbidden
a) enticing
b) prohibited
c) dangerous
d) frightening

17. anxiously
a) sadly
b) angrily
c) worriedly
d) disgustedly

18. cherished
a) holy
b) valuable
c) treasured
d) sentimental

19. devoutly
a) slowly
b) diligently
c) regularly
d) piously

20. bounds
a) limits
b) belief
c) levels
d) patience

The Lady
Comes Again

Chapter 3

Text
Pages
18-26

Perfect Score: 100   Score: _____

1. **falsehood**
   a) unwise statement
   b) confusing statement
   c) untrue statement
   d) surprising statement

2. **grim**
   a) selfish
   b) stern
   c) sorrowful
   d) sensible

3. **frantically**
   a) with great concern
   b) in a frenzied manner
   c) angrily
   d) in a mildly worried manner

4. **frame of mind**
   a) decision
   b) attitude
   c) opinion
   d) belief

5. **startled**
   a) dismayed deeply
   b) angered, infuriated
   c) awakened
   d) surprised, shocked

6. **accompany**
   a) lead
   b) assist
   c) go with
   d) follow

7. **neighboring**
   a) neighborly
   b) nearby
   c) distant
   d) famous

8. **lumbering**
   a) heavy and moving clumsily
   b) moving at a steady speed
   c) headed for a sawmill
   d) large and heavy

9. **gaily**
   a) modestly, decently
   b) traditionally, according to custom
   c) simply, in plain garments
   d) in bright, lively colors

10. **peasants**
    a) farmers or workers of low social
       rank
    b) persons of high social rank
    c) lay persons
    d) wealthy merchants

11. **festive**
    a) characterized by peace
    b) characterized by celebration
    c) characterized by relaxation
    d) characterized by prayerfulness

12. **Lisbon**
    a) capital of Spain
    b) capital of Italy
    c) capital of Yugoslavia
    d) capital of Portugal

13. **imparted**
    a) separated
    b) imported
    c) communicated
    d) printed

14. **slyly**
    a) secretively
    b) unwittingly
    c) unwillingly
    d) skillfully

15. **scant**
    a) abundant
    b) sufficient
    c) little
    d) quiet

16. **gracious**
    a) graceful
    b) kind
    c) holy
    d) happy

17. **informed**
    a) gave permission to
    b) made known to
    c) reprimanded
    d) consoled

18. **gaze**
    a) intense glare
    b) kind face
    c) dignified manner
    d) intent look

19. **devotion**
    a) resigned acceptance
    b) love and service
    c) knowledge and understanding
    d) religious association

20. **Immaculate**
    a) free from all problems
    b) free from all contradictions
    c) free from all stains
    d) free from all sorrows

The Message	**Chapter 4**	Text Pages 27-35

Perfect Score: 100　　　　　　　　　　　　　Score: _____

1. **bewilderment**
    a) state of being disgusted
    b) state of being puzzled
    c) state of being oppressed
    d) state of being repulsed

2. **hastened to**
    a) postponed doing
    b) did promptly
    c) loved to do
    d) did in a careful manner

3. **abandon**
    a) punish, chastise
    b) forsake, leave
    c) frighten, scare
    d) distress, cause suffering to

4. **refuge**
    a) place to get answers
    b) place of learning
    c) place of prayer
    d) place of protection

5. **extended**
    a) shone
    b) deepened
    c) stretched out
    d) intensified

6. **confirm**
    a) establish the truth of
    b) inquire as to the truth of
    c) act in accordance with established standards
    d) work together for a common benefit

7. **blasphemy**
    a) talking badly of one's neighbor
    b) act of disrespect toward parents or other lawful authority
    c) act of disobedience to parents or other lawful authority
    d) act of grave disrespect toward God or anything holy

8. ingratitude
   a) sinfulness
   b) obnoxiousness
   c) unthankfulness
   d) willfulness

9. consecutive
   a) following without interruption
   b) not following any particular order
   c) skipping every other one
   d) scheduled in advance

10. meditating
   a) reciting carefully
   b) daydreaming
   c) praying mentally
   d) praying vocally

11. dawned upon
   a) was completely forgotten by
   b) was suddenly understood by
   c) was dutifully memorized by
   d) was faithfully recorded by

12. forlornly
   a) confusedly
   b) intently
   c) feeling deserted
   d) in silence

13. wistfully
   a) yearningly, longingly
   b) in a rude, selfish manner
   c) in a kind, sweet manner
   d) in a frantic, frenzied manner

14. outskirts
   a) most used area
   b) western side
   c) area around the edges
   d) central area

15. babbling
   a) chattering
   b) arguing
   c) gossiping
   d) debating

16. resolutely
   a) hesitantly
   b) silently
   c) arrogantly
   d) decisively

17. pondered
   a) prayed over
   b) considered thoughtfully
   c) worried about
   d) recalled

18. hearty
   a) unrestrained
   b) rude
   c) insincere
   d) mocking

19. scoffed
   a) laughed uproariously
   b) scolded sternly
   c) threatened angrily
   d) expressed scorn and disbelief

20. deceiving
   a) purposely ignoring
   b) purposely harming
   c) purposely misleading
   d) purposely ridiculing

A New
Life

Chapter 5

Text
Pages
36-45

Perfect Score: 100   Score: _____

1. **heedless**
   a) unmindful
   b) mindful
   c) appreciative
   d) unappreciative

2. **resembled**
   a) were similar to
   b) were reminded of
   c) attempted to imitate
   d) represented

3. **damned**
   a) burning
   b) extremely sinful
   c) condemned to Hell
   d) terrified

4. **reverently**
   a) with intense fear
   b) with great earnestness
   c) silently
   d) with holy respect

5. **cease**
   a) take something seriously
   b) procrastinate
   c) stop
   d) continue

6. **illuminated**
   a) made mysterious
   b) lit up
   c) brightened with colors
   d) beautified

7. **persecution**
   a) investigation
   b) lack of faith
   c) unjust treatment
   d) suffering

8. **consecration**
   a) meditation
   b) absolution
   c) reparation
   d) dedication

9. **martyrs**
   a) people who are murdered
   b) people who die for what is right
   c) people who suffer unjustly
   d) people who suffer in war

10. **conceded**
    a) granted
    b) required
    c) revealed
    d) responded

11. **dogma**
    a) a fact explained by a scholar
    b) a comment made by the Pope
    c) a strong religious belief
    d) a truth proclaimed by the Church

12. **revelation**
    a) will of God
    b) truth made known
    c) holy command
    d) spirituality

13. **befall**
    a) happen to
    b) concern
    c) come forth from
    d) pass by

14. **condemn**
    a) sentence
    b) deserve
    c) terrify
    d) attack

15. **mocking**
    a) gossiping
    b) interfering
    c) announcing
    d) ridiculing

16. **indignation**
    a) strong fear
    b) righteous anger
    c) complete astonishment
    d) lack of dignity

17. (tongues) **wagged**
    a) spoke
    b) argued
    c) chattered
    d) protested

18. **milling about**
    a) moving patiently
    b) moving aimlessly
    c) lining up
    d) gathering in groups

19. **sympathizing with**
    a) assisting, helping
    b) feeling compassion for
    c) being indifferent to
    d) giving advice to

20. **disgrace**
    a) inconvenience
    b) discontent
    c) dishonor
    d) disability

An Unexpected
Journey

Chapter 6

Text
Pages
46-54

Perfect Score: 100

Score: _____

1. **atheists**
    a) persons who claim there is no God
    b) persons who leave the Catholic Faith
    c) persons who believe in God but are
        not Christian
    d) persons who claim they do not know
        whether or not there is a God

2. **bluntly**
    a) harshly and angrily
    b) abruptly and frankly
    c) with indifference
    d) slyly

3. **precautions**
    a) measures taken to control damage
        that has been done
    b) measures taken in advance to
        quicken a task or procedure
    c) measures taken in advance to
        prevent possible harm
    d) measures taken to deceive people

4. **stock**
    a) ancestry
    b) habits
    c) culture
    d) customs

5. **coaxing**
    a) sly manipulation
    b) rough bullying
    c) obvious flattering
    d) gentle persuasion

6. **fraud**
    a) act of disobedience
    b) attempt to stir up trouble
    c) attempt to make money
    d) trickery, deception

7. **rival**
    a) ruin the reputation of
    b) help to publicize
    c) compete with
    d) surpass

8. **prominence**
   a) notability, fame
   b) political power
   c) glory, grandeur
   d) money, wealth

9. **crafty**
   a) angry, furious
   b) intelligent, smart
   c) mean, unkind
   d) cunning, sly

10. **dispatched**
    a) delivered
    b) sent off
    c) ordered
    d) required

11. **summons**
    a) call or command to be present
    b) warning
    c) message from the government
    d) command from the government

12. **advised**
    a) counseled
    b) argued with
    c) persuaded
    d) ordered

13. **imploringly**
    a) courteously
    b) pleadingly
    c) persistently
    d) gravely

14. **in vain**
    a) without knowledge
    b) without preparation
    c) without patience
    d) without success

15. **futile**
    a) persistent, continuing
    b) unimportant, trivial
    c) excessive, exaggerated
    d) ineffective, useless

16. **avail**
    a) appeal or request
    b) harm or hurt
    c) use or profit
    d) meaning or significance

17. **hysterics**
    a) uncontrolled emotional outbursts
    b) insanity
    c) profound meditative prayer
    d) profoundly felt emotions

18. **gleam**
    a) envious look
    b) pained look
    c) disgusted look
    d) crafty look

19. **assure**
    a) announce publicly or formally
    b) try to convince
    c) make an empty promise
    d) deny completely

20. **imposing**
    a) historic
    b) impressive
    c) foreboding
    d) official

Chapter 7

Perfect Score: 100   Score: _____

1. **dismay**
   a) perplexity and puzzlement
   b) annoyance and vexation
   c) scorn and disdain
   d) dejection and fear

2. **jeered**
   a) encouraged
   b) ridiculed
   c) laughed
   d) shouted

3. **pickpockets**
   a) persons who steal from others'
      pockets or purses
   b) persons who cheat others out of their
      money
   c) persons who commit small crimes
   d) tailors who charge high prices to
      repair pockets

4. **bearing**
   a) manner and behavior
   b) gracious manner and behavior
   c) rude manner and behavior
   d) manner of speaking

5. **dismal**
   a) filthy
   b) cramped
   c) gloomy
   d) bare

6. **solemn**
   a) depressed, miserable
   b) grave, serious
   c) distressed, troubled
   d) ardent, fervent

7. **trebles**
   a) melodious voices or sounds
   b) harmonious voices or sounds
   c) low-pitched voices or sounds
   d) high-pitched voices or sounds

8. **faltering**
   a) moving or speaking energetically
   b) moving or speaking roughly
   c) moving or speaking unsteadily
   d) moving or speaking quietly

9. **motley**
   a) diversified, miscellaneous-looking
   b) intimidating, fearsome
   c) irreligious, faithless
   d) deeply impressed

10. **appeased**
    a) brought to a state of anger
    b) brought to a state of joy
    c) brought to a state of calm
    d) brought to a state of justice

11. **recreation**
    a) a type of dance
    b) recovery from illness
    c) enjoyable relaxation
    d) avoidance of responsibility

12. **fumed**
    a) threatened
    b) said with excited irritation
    c) said with bewilderment
    d) showed force

13. **living quarters**
    a) housing accommodations
    b) methods of transportation
    c) private property
    d) places to visit

14. presently
a) now or soon
b) in the far future
c) in the recent past
d) repeatedly

15. twilight
a) bright noonday light
b) dim light before nightfall
c) starlight
d) moonlight

16. gloatingly
a) in a sneaky manner
b) in an angry manner
c) in an intimidating manner
d) with evil satisfaction

17. entrusted
a) concealed
b) placed in someone's care
c) had faith in
d) explained the meaning of

18. listlessly
a) without fear
b) without enthusiasm
c) with anxiety
d) thoughtlessly

19. briskly
a) loudly, forcefully
b) maliciously, hatefully
c) quickly, energetically
d) deceptively, deceitfully

20. strain
a) sorrow
b) pain
c) fear
d) stress

The Fourth Visit	**Chapter 8**	Text Pages 64-73

Perfect Score: 100   Score: _____

1. heartfelt
a) sincere
b) holy
c) fearful
d) silent

2. beloved
a) respected
b) admired
c) cherished
d) needed

3. hustling
a) moving someone steadily
b) moving someone roughly or hurriedly
c) moving someone gently or courteously
d) moving someone uneasily or hesitantly

4. readjust
a) reform
b) realize
c) renew
d) re-adapt

5. depositing
   a) delivering and leaving
   b) banishing
   c) meeting and picking up
   d) abandoning

6. amid
   a) aside from
   b) among
   c) because of
   d) in spite of

7. bombshell (figurative meaning)
   a) news that has a sensational effect
   b) news that starts a fight or argument
   c) news that leaves everyone
      indifferent
   d) news of a violent happening

8. stern
   a) without love
   b) strict and uncompromising
   c) having little trust
   d) having little faith

9. scruples
   a) anxious doubts
   b) feelings of resentment
   c) suspicions
   d) feelings of disgust

10. sensible
   a) highly educated
   b) having a pure heart
   c) having a clear conscience
   d) having good judgment

11. absence
   a) state of being away
   b) state of being needed
   c) state of being nearby
   d) state of being imprisoned

12. atmosphere
   a) a surrounding or dominant odor
   b) a surrounding or dominant mood
   c) the focus of attention
   d) the dominant topic of discussion

13. radiant
   a) causing a glare
   b) shining
   c) well-lit
   d) white

14. vigorously
   a) hurriedly, impatiently
   b) proudly, arrogantly
   c) energetically, forcefully
   d) joyfully, happily

15. grave
   a) exhausted-looking
   b) sincere
   c) serious
   d) cautious

16. conduct
   a) rude thought, word or deed
   b) sinful behavior
   c) behavior
   d) problem

17. sufficient
   a) excessive, extravagant
   b) adequate, enough
   c) scarce, less than enough
   d) a great quantity, much

18. procession
   a) a group of persons walking in the
      same direction
   b) a group of persons gathered together
      for a ceremony
   c) a line of persons standing still
   d) a line of persons walking in a
      ceremonious manner

19. preceding
   a) alongside of
   b) coming before
   c) in the middle of
   d) coming after

20. rapt
   a) melancholy, sad
   b) totally bewildered
   c) wholly absorbed
   d) listless, apathetic

New Crowds
in the Cova

Chapter 9

Text
Pages
74-83

Perfect Score: 100   Score: _____

1. **fragrance**
   a) decoration
   b) flavor
   c) ornament
   d) scent

2. **hitherto**
   a) a long time ago
   b) at the present time
   c) up to now
   d) from now on

3. **idle**
   a) evil
   b) stupid
   c) useless
   d) humorous

4. **laden**
   a) overcome
   b) burdened
   c) disappointed
   d) sorrowing

5. **manifest**
   a) renew
   b) show
   c) humble
   d) devote

6. **majestically**
   a) in a royal manner
   b) graciously or sweetly
   c) beautifully
   d) in a graceful manner

7. **hazarded**
   a) ventured
   b) denied
   c) disregarded
   d) confirmed

8. **publicity**
   a) idle talk or rumors
   b) spreading of information
   c) newspaper articles
   d) announcements by loud speaker

9. **gnarled**
   a) smooth
   b) knotted
   c) emaciated
   d) hard

10. **piped**
    a) spoke in a melodious tone
    b) spoke in an exasperated tone
    c) spoke in a high-pitched tone
    d) spoke in a low-pitched tone

11. **steadfastly**
    a) unwaveringly
    b) briefly but certainly
    c) honestly
    d) spontaneously

12. **supernatural**
    a) superstitious
    b) pertaining to God
    c) pertaining to human nature
    d) mysterious

13. **conspirators**
    a) partners in an important or urgent
       project
    b) persons cooperating together to carry
       out a business plan
    c) persons joining in a secret agreement
       to do a wrongful act
    d) any criminals

14. **scheme**
    a) plan, plot
    b) goal, end
    c) effect, result
    d) program, schedule

15. **pilgrimage**
    a) penitential act
    b) religious journey
    c) religious procession
    d) recitation of prayers

16. **emphatically**
    a) forcefully
    b) confidentially
    c) inquiringly
    d) wisely

17. **prudent**
    a) secretive in practical affairs
    b) opinionated in practical affairs
    c) timid in practical affairs
    d) wise in practical affairs

18. **inquiry**
    a) investigation
    b) judgment
    c) debate
    d) opposition

19. **theology**
    a) the study of theories
    b) the study of philosophy
    c) the study of therapy
    d) the study of God

20. **seminary**
    a) place of burial
    b) college where priests teach
    c) place of retreat for priests
    d) school to prepare men for the priesthood

| The Great Miracle | **Chapter 10** | Text Pages 84-95 |

Perfect Score: 100

Score: _____

1. **learned** (adjective)
   a) having much knowledge
   b) very intelligent
   c) teaching
   d) holding a college degree

2. **prophecy**
   a) prayer
   b) foretelling
   c) story
   d) report

3. **throng**
   a) impatient crowd
   b) group of adults
   c) large crowd
   d) waiting crowd

4. **inspiration**
   a) idea or impulse that comes to one
   b) idea or plan that one has formed by oneself
   c) religious plan
   d) plan of action, strategy

5. **supplication**
   a) truthful statement
   b) humble petition
   c) hopeful waiting
   d) detailed meditation

6. **vigil**
   a) a period of watching and praying, especially at night
   b) a period of time spent in reading and study
   c) a period of strenuous manual labor
   d) a period of prayer and fasting

7. **marvel**
   a) something arousing religious fervor
   b) something arousing astonishment
   c) something arousing confidence
   d) something quelling fear

8. **plea**
   a) desire
   b) appeal
   c) persuasion
   d) question

9. **instilled**
   a) prepared
   b) put into
   c) drawn out of
   d) educated

10. **ominous**
    a) omnipresent
    b) foreboding
    c) mysterious
    d) tragic

11. **impelled**
    a) driven
    b) struck
    c) dispersed
    d) affected

12. **shafts**
    a) particles
    b) brightness
    c) beams
    d) flames

13. **spellbound**
    a) bored, indifferent
    b) distressed, alarmed
    c) inspired, exalted
    d) entranced, fascinated

14. **spectacle**
    a) occurrence
    b) event
    c) exhibition
    d) announcement

15. **myriad**
    a) colorful display
    b) circular display
    c) somewhat large number
    d) immense number

16. **revolving**
    a) moving unsteadily
    b) shaking
    c) moving in circles
    d) moving up and down

17. **mass**
    a) a small number
    b) a large, tightly packed group
    c) a medium-sized group
    d) a set or determined number

18. **garbed**
    a) decorated
    b) fashioned
    c) adorned
    d) clothed

19. **contrary**
    a) unfamiliar
    b) opposite
    c) different
    d) new

20. **nestling**
    a) sleeping, resting
    b) being carried
    c) being loved
    d) settling snugly

The
Victims

Chapter 11

Text
Pages
96-107

Perfect Score: 100   Score: _____

1. **normalcy**
   a) usualness
   b) boredom
   c) legality
   d) peace

2. **tuberculosis**
   a) disease that especially affects the
      digestive system
   b) disease that causes loss of memory
   c) disease that especially affects the
      heart
   d) disease that especially affects the
      lungs

3. **ailment**
   a) feeling
   b) situation
   c) condition
   d) illness

4. **stupendous**
   a) famous
   b) causing astonishment
   c) outrageous
   d) causing great joy

5. **malice**
   a) superstition
   b) atheism
   c) ill will
   d) anger

6. **astray**
   a) away from what is common
   b) away from what is right
   c) away from what is known
   d) away from what is easy

7. **superstitious**
   a) believing in magic or charms
   b) full of piety, religious devotion
   c) timid, lacking in self-confidence
   d) stupid

8. **unleashed**
   a) dispersed
   b) let loose
   c) established
   d) put into effect

9. **had forfeited**
   a) had rejected
   b) had forsaken
   c) had refused the use of
   d) had lost the right to

10. **conceited**
    a) having too low an opinion of oneself
    b) having too high an opinion of
       oneself
    c) having too low an opinion of others
    d) having too high an opinion of others

11. **spin**
    a) make fibers out of thread
    b) make cloth on a loom
    c) make thread out of fibers
    d) sew clothing out of fabric

12. **cutting** (remarks)
    a) hurtful
    b) annoying
    c) misunderstood
    d) dishonest

13. persevere
a) persist despite obstacles
b) do something with good intentions
c) preserve
d) honestly try to accomplish something

14. mortifications
a) acts of self-denial
b) acts of obedience
c) acts of faith
d) acts of charity

15. extreme
a) extra
b) excessive
c) unknown
d) customary

16. rigorous
a) merciless
b) painful
c) strict
d) humble

17. victim
a) one who suffers on behalf of others
b) one who suffers to make up for one's own sins
c) one who prays for sinners
d) one who practices prayer and fasting

18. anticipated
a) predicted
b) warned
c) expected
d) planned

19. penitential
a) joyful
b) pessimistic
c) atoning
d) prayerful

20. placidly
a) sweetly
b) resolutely
c) wisely
d) calmly

The Bells Toll in Fatima	# Chapter 12	Text Pages 108-119

Perfect Score: 100   **Score: _____**

1. foreseen
a) known in advance or expected
b) informed, told
c) feared, dreaded
d) desired to happen

2. consumed with
a) constantly discussing
b) interested in
c) obnoxious about
d) engrossed with

3. latter
a) the first of two mentioned
b) the second of two mentioned
c) the older of two mentioned
d) the younger of two mentioned

4. dumbfounded
a) rather surprised
b) ignorant or uninformed
c) speechless with amazement
d) filled with wonder and joy

5. indefinite
   a) extremely long
   b) clearly determined
   c) not clearly determined
   d) short

6. splendid
   a) magnificent
   b) devout
   c) useful
   d) spiritual

7. erect
   a) make plans for
   b) get permission for
   c) raise money for
   d) build

8. plague
   a) dangerous, contagious disease
   b) famine
   c) destructive war
   d) destructive storm

9. suspended
   a) stopped for a time
   b) fixed or repaired
   c) cancelled permanently
   d) rescheduled

10. tolled
   a) sounded unceasingly
   b) sounded with slow, measured strokes, as for a funeral
   c) sounded with loud, blaring tones
   d) sounded with high-pitched tones

11. requiem
   a) music or Church service
   b) music or Church service for the sick
   c) music or Church service for sinners
   d) music or Church service for the dead

12. malady
   a) malfunction
   b) starvation
   c) suffering
   d) disease

13. perplexed
   a) bothered
   b) worried
   c) terrified
   d) puzzled

14. speculated
   a) prophesied
   b) understood
   c) made guesses
   d) feared

15. invalids
   a) persons suffering from the plague
   b) persons too sick or weak to care for themselves
   c) persons who are depressed
   d) persons too poor to care for themselves

16. ardently
   a) wistfully
   b) attentively
   c) excitedly
   d) fervently

17. merit
   a) deserve by God's grace
   b) believe by God's grace
   c) discover by God's grace
   d) foresee by God's grace

18. convalescing
   a) recovering one's health
   b) taking precautions to avoid getting sick
   c) being cared for during an illness
   d) losing health and strength during an illness

19. confided
   a) entrusted someone with a secret
   b) spoke in a low tone of voice
   c) deliberated matters carefully
   d) loyally kept a secret

20. wasted
   a) old and worn out
   b) diseased
   c) thin and worn out
   d) infected

The Great
Sacrifice

Chapter 13

Text
Pages
120-130

Perfect Score: 100   Score: _____

1. **fitful**
   a) restless, spasmodic
   b) fussy, finicky
   c) calm, peaceful
   d) painful

2. **vent**
   a) declaration
   b) revelation
   c) release
   d) restriction

3. **grieving**
   a) feeling sorrow
   b) feeling gratitude
   c) feeling anger
   d) feeling a loss of control

4. **succeeded**
   a) came before
   b) passed by slowly
   c) followed after
   d) occurred at the same time as

5. **stricken with**
   a) discovered with
   b) afflicted with
   c) dismayed by
   d) suffering from

6. **influenza**
   a) contagious disease that especially
      affects the bone structure
   b) contagious disease that especially
      affects the circulatory system
   c) contagious disease that especially
      affects the respiratory system
   d) contagious disease that especially
      affects the nervous system

7. **pleurisy**
   a) a spinal disorder
   b) a heart disorder
   c) a lung disorder
   d) a brain disorder

8. **abscess**
   a) large open wound
   b) mass of blood in a body tissue
   c) mass of pus in a body tissue
   d) pocket of water in a body tissue

9. **soberly**
   a) very nonchalantly
   b) very knowingly
   c) very miserably
   d) very seriously

10. **regarded**
    a) looked at
    b) enjoyed the company of
    c) held a conversation with
    d) listened to

11. **conviction**
    a) feeling of fear
    b) feeling of sorrow
    c) feeling of certainty
    d) concern

12. **overpowering**
    a) eternal
    b) overwhelming
    c) horrifying
    d) profound

13. **grasp**
    a) comprehend
    b) learn
    c) consider
    d) analyze

14. refrained from
a) commanded not to
b) encouraged not to
c) volunteered not to
d) kept oneself from

15. deprive of
a) offer up
b) maintain
c) suffer
d) withhold

16. merits
a) claims to spiritual reward
b) spiritual abilities
c) prayers
d) spiritual responsibilities

17. tone
a) impulse
b) ability
c) outlook
d) character

18. surpassed
a) exceeded
b) equalled
c) rivalled
d) increased

19. ordeal
a) long and unpleasant journey
b) very painful experience
c) painful medical procedure
d) tragic, distressing news

20. vision
a) something mysterious that is heard
b) something mysterious that is pondered
c) something mysterious that is seen
d) something mysterious that is meditated upon

To Lisbon

Chapter 14

Text Pages 131-142

Perfect Score: 100

Score: _____

1. distressing
a) causing anxiety or pain
b) causing boredom or listlessness
c) causing perplexity or bewilderment
d) causing astonishment

2. expenses
a) details
b) budgets
c) costs
d) financial planning

3. foretold
a) foreshadowed
b) warned
c) predicted
d) informed

4. well-nigh
a) very quickly
b) certainly
c) inevitably
d) almost

5. wanly
a) sweetly
b) respectfully
c) feebly
d) uncooperatively

6. had recourse to
a) chose
b) turned to for help
c) inquired into the meaning of
d) returned to

7. **vow**
   a) sacrament
   b) solemn promise
   c) devout meditation
   d) religious practice

8. **secular**
   a) anti-religious
   b) not concerned with duty
   c) immodest
   d) non-religious

9. **reverenced**
   a) prayed sincerely for
   b) obeyed with swiftness
   c) regarded with affection
   d) regarded with holy respect

10. **sanctuary**
    a) part of a church where the high altar stands
    b) part of a church where priests vest
    c) part of a church next to the bell tower
    d) platform from which the priest delivers sermons

11. **piety**
    a) devotion to God
    b) love of neighbor
    c) virtue
    d) zeal for souls

12. **considerable**
    a) indefinite amount or degree
    b) small amount or degree
    c) fairly large amount or degree
    d) in great detail

13. **precision**
    a) maturity
    b) exactness
    c) knowledge
    d) experience

14. **matter-of-fact**
    a) informative
    b) unemotional
    c) inquisitive
    d) grave

15. **liberty**
    a) justice
    b) power
    c) authority
    d) freedom

16. **inspiring**
    a) uplifting
    b) serious
    c) instructive
    d) comforting

17. **intensity**
    a) variety
    b) definiteness, precision
    c) force, severity
    d) pain, suffering

18. **anguish**
    a) inflammation
    b) injury
    c) infection
    d) suffering

19. **evading**
    a) obeying
    b) avoiding
    c) forgetting
    d) denying

20. **incredulously**
    a) with disbelief
    b) with sympathy
    c) with worry
    d) with suffering

Perfect Score: 100   Score: _____

1. **consolation**
   a) something that brings sorrow
   b) something that challenges
   c) something that enlightens, informs
   d) something that gives cheer or lessens sorrow

2. **mortal**
   a) subject to death
   b) funeral
   c) buried
   d) subject to a life of poverty

3. **remains**
   a) casket, coffin
   b) body after the soul has left
   c) invalid
   d) soul after the body has died

4. **evident**
   a) genuine, honest
   b) visible, clearly seen
   c) enthusiastic, eager
   d) expressive

5. **subscription**
   a) signed pledges to make contributions
   b) money raised through taxation
   c) approval by legitimate authority
   d) perseverance in a good work

6. **stamped out**
   a) omitted
   b) destroyed
   c) approved
   d) rejected

7. **hysterical**
   a) deceived, fooled
   b) crippled, disabled
   c) excessively emotional
   d) deceitful, dishonest

8. **proclaimed**
   a) confided
   b) declared openly
   c) promised
   d) commanded publicly

9. **insinuated**
   a) rashly judged
   b) inserted by force
   c) inserted subtly
   d) confused

10. **observance**
    a) prohibition, banning
    b) commemoration, celebration
    c) announcement, publicity
    d) pilgrimage or procession

11. **well-founded**
    a) based on sincere desires
    b) based on optimistic hopes
    c) based on good judgment
    d) based on strong opinion

12. **deterred**
    a) prevented from acting
    b) assisted, helped
    c) annoyed, pestered
    d) worried

13. **tribute**
    a) act or gift to aid the poor
    b) act or gift expressing mourning
    c) act or gift in atonement
    d) act or gift giving honor to someone

14. **recitation**
    a) meditation
    b) repeating aloud from memory
    c) singing
    d) reading aloud from a script

15. **at the beck and call of**
    a) the topic of gossip by
    b) commanded to serve
    c) subject to harsh treatment from
    d) subject to every request of

16. **was conducted**
    a) was commanded
    b) was founded
    c) was cultivated
    d) was run

17. **unwittingly**
    a) unwillingly
    b) unknowingly
    c) undeniably
    d) unconsolably

18. **porous**
    a) heavy
    b) green
    c) dense
    d) not dense

19. **adjoining**
    a) bordering
    b) diagonal from
    c) surrounding
    d) included with

20. **venerated**
    a) believed in
    b) consecrated
    c) sanctified
    d) honored

Instructions: Circle the letter of the answer which best matches the meaning of the vocabulary word.

Shepherd Boy	**Chapter 1**	Text Pages 1-10

Perfect Score: 100   Score: _____

1. **withhold**
   a) conceal from view
   b) withstand
   c) refrain from giving
   d) hinder from attaining

2. **obtain**
   a) imitate
   b) acquire
   c) learn
   d) receive

3. **outwit**
   a) outsmart
   b) outweigh
   c) outwork
   d) destroy

4. **tilled**
   a) built upon
   b) cultivated
   c) landscaped
   d) harvested

5. **spared**
   a) ordered to carry out
   b) loaded down with
   c) beaten
   d) freed up

6. **accompanied**
   a) assisted
   b) went along with
   c) helped
   d) followed

7. **acknowledged**
   a) denied the truth of
   b) made clear the truth of
   c) became aware of the truth of
   d) professed the truth of

8. **uphold**
   a) improve
   b) support
   c) admire
   d) analyze

9. **peddlers**
   a) persons who are homeless
   b) persons who preach from door to door
   c) persons who sell from door to door
   d) burglars who go from house to house

10. **makeshift**
   a) broken-down
   b) rickety, flimsy
   c) hidden, disguised
   d) temporary, homemade

11. consolation
  a) something that causes surprise and wonder
  b) something that gives comfort and strength
  c) something that requires strength and courage
  d) something that is done in secrecy

12. supernatural
  a) pertaining to God
  b) inspiring
  c) philosophical
  d) pertaining to superstition

13. channels (literal meaning)
  a) reservoirs, tanks
  b) places, rooms
  c) waterways, canals
  d) oceans, seas

14. profess
  a) declare openly
  b) speak loudly
  c) believe firmly
  d) trust constantly

15. partnership
  a) vocation, calling
  b) high ideal
  c) effort shared by two persons
  d) understanding between two persons

16. presented
  a) introduced
  b) emphasized
  c) detected
  d) accomplished

17. coaxing
  a) attempting to influence by trickery, deceit
  b) attempting to move by force
  c) attempting to discourage
  d) attempting to influence by gentle persuasion

18. pastime
  a) game of make-believe
  b) recreation, amusement
  c) outdoor activity
  d) devotional practice

19. persecution
  a) unjust treatment
  b) hardship
  c) suffering
  d) just punishment

20. exile
  a) imprisonment
  b) hiding
  c) banishment
  d) execution

The Struggle Begins	# Chapter 2	Text Pages 11-20

Perfect Score: 100   **Score:** _____

1. pruned
  a) covered over the roots of
  b) picked the ripe fruits of
  c) pulled up weeds around
  d) cut off excess branches of

2. was inclined
  a) started
  b) was eager
  c) was reluctant
  d) tended

3. **procedure**
   a) style of behavior
   b) schedule of events
   c) set of events
   d) method of action

4. **pomp**
   a) peace, silence
   b) devotion, prayerfulness
   c) splendid display
   d) careful attention to details

5. **crisis**
   a) emergency
   b) shortage
   c) challenge
   d) adventure

6. **conducted**
   a) inspired
   b) commanded, ordered
   c) instigated, provoked
   d) led, directed

7. **longingly**
   a) with desire
   b) with insistence
   c) with impatience
   d) with envy

8. **lukewarm**
   a) serene
   b) mild-mannered
   c) half-hearted
   d) malicious

9. **theology**
   a) the study of Angels and anything pertaining to them
   b) the study of God and anything pertaining to Him
   c) the study of various religions
   d) the study of Church ceremonies

10. **candidate for** (something)
    a) member of
    b) possible future member of
    c) definite future member of
    d) former member of

11. **notions**
    a) advice
    b) ideas
    c) plans
    d) objections

12. **reproachfully**
    a) with anger and vengefulness
    b) with disapproval and criticism
    c) with annoyance and irritation
    d) with sorrow and grief

13. **dowry**
    a) money or goods that a bride brings to her husband at marriage
    b) money or goods that a bride gives to the poor to celebrate her marriage
    c) money or goods that a bride needs in order to pay for her wedding
    d) money or goods that a bride gives to her parents at her wedding

14. **expense**
    a) cost
    b) budget
    c) bother
    d) money

15. **overcome**
    a) predicted
    b) conquered
    c) ignored
    d) made light of

16. **viewpoint**
    a) objection
    b) worry
    c) opinion
    d) knowledge

17. **justifiable**
    a) unfortunate
    b) expected
    c) reasonable
    d) irrational

18. **absorbed in**
    a) completely freed from
    b) deeply interested or involved in
    c) invited to take part in
    d) commanded to take part in

19. **down-hearted**
    a) confused
    b) rebellious
    c) exasperated
    d) dejected

20. **abruptly**
    a) suddenly
    b) aggravatedly
    c) slowly
    d) graciously

The Struggle
Continues

Chapter 3

Perfect Score: 100   Score: _____

1. **prevailed upon**
   a) politely requested
   b) hinted or suggested
   c) succeeded in persuading
   d) offered encouragement to

2. **missionary**
   a) one who lives in a monastery
   b) one who is an expert in theology
   c) one who does work in a foreign land
   d) one who is sent somewhere to
      teach about God

3. **remorse**
   a) regret for wrongdoing
   b) sadness at having been offended
   c) kindness
   d) embarrassment

4. **earnestly**
   a) with kindness and consideration
   b) somberly
   c) slowly and deliberately
   d) with heartfelt sincerity

5. **wretched**
   a) shocking, frightening
   b) undesirable in any way
   c) very distressing, miserable
   d) violent

6. **venture**
   a) difficult or risky undertaking
   b) poorly thought-out plan
   c) foolish undertaking
   d) act of pride

7. **woebegone**
   a) looking ashamed
   b) looking miserable
   c) looking fearful
   d) having a blank look

8. **faltered**
   a) changed
   b) suggested
   c) hesitated
   d) blushed

9. **mortifications**
   a) acts of faith
   b) acts of self-denial
   c) public acts of penance
   d) liturgical devotions

10. **solely**
    a) especially
    b) specifically
    c) only
    d) probably

11. **graces**
   a) supernatural helps
   b) prayers to the Saints
   c) merits
   d) mortifications

12. **tramp**
   a) traveling beggar
   b) disabled beggar
   c) burglar
   d) person who refuses to work

13. **ministered to**
   a) cared for, especially spiritually
   b) cared for, especially secretly
   c) cared for, especially in danger
   d) cared for heroically

14. **peril**
   a) doubt
   b) persecution
   c) danger
   d) offense

15. **merit**
   a) petition
   b) induce
   c) accomplish
   d) deserve

16. **perseverance**
   a) strength
   b) persistence
   c) stubbornness
   d) confidence

17. **imprudent**
   a) spontaneous
   b) unwise in practical affairs
   c) disobedient in practical affairs
   d) judgmental

18. **goodly**
   a) of a specified size or amount
   b) of a large size or amount
   c) of a desired size or amount
   d) of an unexpected size or amount

19. **ambitions**
   a) desires to achieve some goal
   b) foolish daydreams
   c) efforts, labors
   d) difficulties, frustrations

20. **summons**
   a) a call by authority to withdraw
   b) a call by authority to appear
   c) a command to begin doing something
   d) a command to cease doing something

Escape | **Chapter 4** | Text Pages 32-43

Perfect Score: 100   Score: _____

1. **strict**
   a) loose
   b) precise
   c) religious
   d) scholastic

2. **omitted**
   a) forgotten
   b) neglected
   c) left out
   d) cancelled

3. (army) **detachment**
   a) group of soldiers sent on a
       particular mission
   b) group of soldiers assigned to do
       maintenance work
   c) group of military officers
   d) group of soldiers recovering from
       illness or injury

4. preliminary
a) final
b) heartfelt
c) difficult
d) preparatory

5. resignation
a) an accepting attitude
b) a sorrowful attitude
c) a snobbish attitude
d) an enthusiastic attitude

6. dismay
a) sudden, strong anger
b) sudden, intense disappointment
c) sudden, overwhelming joy
d) any sudden feeling

7. twilight
a) broad daylight
b) moonlight
c) evening light
d) starlight

8. frontier
a) capital
b) border
c) war
d) battlefield

9. recruit
a) someone thinking about joining the armed forces
b) newly enlisted member of the armed forces
c) someone who has been in the armed forces for a year or more
d) officer in the armed forces

10. to report
a) to present oneself
b) to find fault with
c) to fail to show up
d) to carry out an assignment

11. seized
a) shoved suddenly or forcibly
b) squeezed suddenly or forcibly
c) hit or struck suddenly or forcibly
d) took hold of suddenly or forcibly

12. deserters
a) those who enter military service late
b) those who leave military service permanently with permission
c) those who leave military service permanently without permission
d) those who are expelled from military service

13. towering
a) reaching a great height
b) fuming and sputtering
c) frowning fiercely
d) poised to strike

14. conscious
a) dazed
b) fatigued
c) conscience-stricken
d) aware

15. hoisted
a) lifted
b) positioned
c) arranged
d) swung

16. vaguely
a) unpredictably
b) indistinctly
c) with surprise
d) with fear

17. dense
a) high
b) dark
c) closely compacted
d) large and intimidating

18. disgrace
a) loss of faith
b) loss of comfort
c) loss of honor
d) loss of support

VOCABULARY QUIZ WORKBOOK

19. **benefactor**
    a) one who hides another
    b) one who lives in the forest
    c) one who punishes
    d) one who gives aid

20. **frantically**
    a) desperately, wildly
    b) stubbornly, persistently
    c) secretly, stealthily
    d) energetically, vigorously

A New
Decision

Chapter 5

Text
Pages
44-53

Perfect Score: 100

Score: _____

1. **clambered**
    a) pulled oneself upward
    b) walked up an incline
    c) climbed awkwardly
    d) climbed with ease

2. **stifling**
    a) suffocating
    b) unpleasant
    c) small
    d) hot

3. **deferred**
    a) cancelled
    b) detained
    c) postponed
    d) desisted

4. **departure**
    a) leaving
    b) announcing that one is going to leave
    c) absence
    d) travel

5. **marred**
    a) prevented
    b) enhanced
    c) ended
    d) spoiled

6. **tributes**
    a) words or gifts that express sorrow
    b) words or gifts that give consolation
    c) words or gifts that give honor
    d) any words or gifts

7. **unduly**
    a) excessively
    b) sorrowfully
    c) understandingly
    d) undutifully

8. **forlorn**
    a) weak and hungry
    b) miserable and alone
    c) tired and exhausted
    d) desperate

9. **capacity**
    a) basement, cellar
    b) position, role
    c) apartment
    d) salary, pay

10. **sacristan**
    a) one who opens a church in the morning and locks it up at night
    b) one who distributes alms to the poor
    c) one who does maintenance work at church
    d) one who cares for the altar and vestments

11. **handyman**
    a) man who does odd jobs
    b) driver, chauffeur
    c) cook, chef
    d) groundskeeper, landscaper

12. mortified
    a) devoted to the will of God
    b) having spent years in the practice
       of meditation
    c) having mastered one's self-will
       by self-discipline
    d) having received special graces

13. vanities
    a) things that are expensive
    b) things that are spiritually worthless
    c) things that bring pleasure
    d) things that are sinful

14. be abandoned to
    a) have complete permission to
    b) surrender oneself to
    c) be totally sure of
    d) take what belongs to oneself

15. be entitled to
    a) receive as a gift
    b) have a right to
    c) be required to
    d) be forbidden to

16. distinction
    a) distinguishing mark
    b) beneficial quality
    c) ability
    d) knowledge

17. keep abreast of
    a) fall behind in
    b) get ahead of
    c) keep up with
    d) excel in

18. keen (literal meaning)
    a) heavy
    b) large
    c) sharp
    d) bright

19. designs
    a) power, might
    b) commandments, laws
    c) holiness, sanctity
    d) purposes, plans

20. pondered
    a) appreciated
    b) desired
    c) considered
    d) believed in

Back To Work   # Chapter 6   Text Pages 54-63

Perfect Score: 100   Score: _____

1. novitiate
    a) place to prepare to take the vows
       of religious life
    b) place to prepare for the priesthood
    c) home for elderly members of a
       religious order
    d) place to learn to teach catechism

2. without more ado
    a) without much hope
    b) without further delay
    c) without permission
    d) without taking along any money

3. emphatic
   a) enthusiastic
   b) forceful
   c) angry
   d) thoughtful

4. unflinchingly
   a) without faltering
   b) without caring
   c) timidly
   d) searchingly

5. had commenced
   a) had decided to begin
   b) had finished
   c) had begun
   d) had planned

6. subdeacon
   a) man who has received Minor Orders
      as a step to the priesthood
   b) seminarian who studies philosophy
      and theology
   c) priest who helps the Bishop or
      Archbishop
   d) student preparing to enter the
      seminary

7. valiant
   a) foolishly daring
   b) presumptuous
   c) boldly courageous
   d) selflessly generous

8. trifle
   a) little bit
   b) very
   c) unusually
   d) doubly

9. irregular
   a) unusual, abnormal
   b) senseless, foolish
   c) distressing, causing pain
   d) inconvenient, annoying

10. learned
   a) very intelligent
   b) having much knowledge
   c) having a great desire for knowledge
   d) having good judgment

11. Vicar General
   a) priest who is pastor of more than
      one parish
   b) priest who may take the place of
      the Bishop
   c) priest who ministers to the Generals
      in the Army
   d) priest who teaches at a seminary or
      Catholic university

12. enlightenment
   a) virtue
   b) hope
   c) mercy
   d) understanding

13. dispensation
   a) exemption from a rule
   b) command from authority
   c) act of obedience
   d) announcement in the newspaper

14. the Revolution
   a) political and religious turmoil in
      France in and around 1789
   b) political and religious turmoil in
      Spain in and around 1789
   c) political and religious turmoil in
      France in and around 1889
   d) political and religious turmoil in
      Spain in and around 1889

15. vice
   a) rowdiness
   b) lack of prayer
   c) poverty
   d) immorality

16. zeal
  a) holy compassion
  b) holy enthusiasm
  c) holy recollection
  d) holy obedience

17. obscure
  a) uneducated
  b) unknown
  c) unpopular
  d) unintelligent

18. overshadowed
  a) brightened, increased
  b) ruined
  c) brought to one's attention
  d) exceeded in importance

19. canon
  a) a priest who has a position at
      the cathedral
  b) a parish priest
  c) a priest who teaches at a seminary
  d) a priest who lives in a monastery

20. gravely
  a) very enthusiatically
  b) with great hesitation
  c) very seriously
  d) with great joy

Farewell
To Ecully

Chapter 7

Perfect Score: 100   **Score:** _____

1. major seminary
  a) school for high-school-age young men
      preparing for the priesthood
  b) school for college-age men
      preparing for the priesthood
  c) very large monastery for religious
      brothers
  d) very large burial field

2. had taken refuge
  a) had hidden from the military
  b) had found protection, safety
  c) had withdrawn from the world
  d) had spent time in prayer

3. pastoral
  a) pertaining to a priest's duties to
      his Bishop
  b) pertaining to a priest's own spiritual
      life
  c) pertaining to a priest's duties to
      his people
  d) pertaining to a priest's relationship
      to his parents

4. tactfully
  a) in a tricky manner
  b) with embarrassment
  c) avoiding giving offense
  d) bashfully

5. assistant
  a) helper
  b) co-worker
  c) brother
  d) student

6. frank
  a) kind and understanding
  b) open and straightforward
  c) meek and humble
  d) discouraged yet hopeful

7. manufacturer
  a) one who makes or produces
      something
  b) one who imports or exports
      something
  c) one who operates any business
  d) one who runs a bank

VOCABULARY QUIZ WORKBOOK

8. **propagation**
   a) support
   b) spread
   c) discussion
   d) study

9. **mastering**
   a) learning thoroughly
   b) becoming used to
   c) becoming extremely fond of
   d) becoming acquainted with

10. **render**
    a) understand
    b) make, give
    c) study, learn
    d) assist, aid

11. **penitent**
    a) person who feels guilty
    b) person who holds a grudge
    c) person who confesses sin
    d) person who commits sin

12. **resolved**
    a) sorry
    b) having a wish
    c) having a weak intent
    d) having a firm intent

13. **sublime**
    a) exalted, glorious
    b) comforting, compassionate
    c) sacramental
    d) forgiving

14. **absolution**
    a) prayers of a priest for a person in Confession
    b) blessing of a priest on a person in Confession
    c) forgiveness of sin by a priest for a person in Confession
    d) advice of a priest to a person in Confession

15. **administered**
    a) prayed, meditated
    b) blessed
    c) performed, dispensed
    d) offered, sacrificed

16. **dialect**
    a) a distinct variety of French
    b) dialogue, conversation
    c) translation of a language
    d) a distinct variety of a language

17. **impulse**
    a) urging
    b) prayer
    c) grace
    d) vision

18. **dilapidated**
    a) unimpressive
    b) unused or empty
    c) old or ancient
    d) in need of repair

19. **thatched**
    a) covered with tile
    b) shabbily made
    c) fragile or delicate
    d) covered with straw

20. **conviction**
    a) imagination
    b) firm belief
    c) persistent thought
    d) general opinion

Sowing
The Seed

Chapter 8

Text
Pages
75-84

Perfect Score: 100   Score: _____

1. a score
   a) 75
   b) 100
   c) 20
   d) 12

2. coarse
   a) crude, vulgar
   b) irreligious
   c) untruthful, deceitful
   d) mean, unkind

3. servile (work)
   a) physical
   b) mental
   c) done for money
   d) disobedient

4. on the slightest provocation
   a) with some degree of anger
   b) with some degree of shame
   c) for very little pay
   d) for very little reason

5. save for
   a) except for
   b) in addition to
   c) along with
   d) in order for

6. pious
   a) kind
   b) honest
   c) intelligent
   d) devout

7. uniting
   a) offering
   b) joining
   c) bringing
   d) leading

8. dire
   a) foolish, silly
   b) expressing extreme annoyance
   c) warning of disaster
   d) expressing anger or fury

9. justified
   a) shown to be wrong
   b) shown to be right
   c) shown to be irrational
   d) shown to be extreme

10. resented
   a) were concerned and worried
   b) were offended and angry
   c) were repentant and contrite
   d) were sorrowful and grief-stricken

11. indignant
   a) unhappy
   b) angry
   c) undignified
   d) worried

12. christening
   a) baptism
   b) confirmation
   c) feast day
   d) any religious occasion

13. squandered
   a) cheated regarding
   b) used selfishly
   c) used wastefully
   d) gambled

14. ancestral
   a) beautifully constructed
   b) having belonged to one's forefathers
   c) artistic
   d) very important in history

15. **profane**
    a) treat with irreverence
    b) publicize
    c) behave irresponsibly toward
    d) forget

16. **confraternity**
    a) any group of people
    b) group of people in France
    c) group of people devoted to religious works
    d) group of people devoted to works of some kind

17. **guild**
    a) any group of people
    b) group of people in France
    c) group of people devoted to religious works
    d) group of people devoted to works of some kind

18. **hazard**
    a) something strange
    b) something embarrassing
    c) something disgraceful
    d) something unsafe

19. **conspicuous**
    a) attracting attention
    b) overly pious
    c) conceited, prideful
    d) silly, ridiculous

20. **unwaveringly**
    a) steadily
    b) compassionately
    c) spiritually
    d) piously

New Trials	# Chapter 9	Text Pages 85-96

Perfect Score: 100   Score: _____

1. **deputation**
    a) group of persons elected by ballot
    b) group of famous or important persons
    c) group of office-holders
    d) group of persons sent on behalf of another

2. **ferry**
    a) boat for transportation across a river
    b) boat for transportation down a river
    c) boat for pleasure trips
    d) large boat for any purpose

3. **rectory**
    a) house where a parish priest lives
    b) house where seminarians live
    c) house where religious brothers live
    d) house where nuns live

4. **triumphantly**
    a) recklessly
    b) exultantly
    c) frantically
    d) in a relieved manner

5. **borne**
    a) charged, billed
    b) accepted, assumed
    c) finished, ended
    d) ignored, evaded

6. **Providence**
    a) the Commandments of God
    b) the Will of God
    c) God's care for His creatures
    d) God's judgment of each person

7. **previous**
   a) before
   b) during
   c) after
   d) later

8. **latter**
   a) the second of two mentioned
   b) the second of three mentioned
   c) the first of two mentioned
   d) the more important of two mentioned

9. **malice**
   a) desire to inflict harm
   b) desire to excite curiosity
   c) desire to gain a selfish advantage
   d) anger

10. **taverns**
    a) stores where alcoholic beverages are sold
    b) places where alcoholic beverages are sold and served
    c) places where gambling takes place
    d) places where dances are held

11. **anonymous**
    a) lacking all courtesy or respect
    b) suspicious
    c) lacking the writer's name
    d) scheming, dishonest

12. **slanderous**
    a) attacking someone's reputation
    b) excited by curiosity
    c) upholding someone's reputation
    d) rejecting wise guidance

13. **withdrawn**
    a) incorporated into
    b) added to
    c) taken away
    d) changed

14. **diocese**
    a) territory under the jurisdiction of a bishop
    b) territory under the jurisdiction of a priest
    c) territory under the jurisdiction of a monsignor
    d) territory under the jurisdiction of an archbishop

15. **archdiocese**
    a) small rural diocese
    b) diocese ruled by an archbishop
    c) large rural diocese
    d) diocese ruled by a bishop

16. **hitherto**
    a) long ago
    b) recently
    c) almost
    d) until now

17. **boarders**
    a) students who live at their school
    b) students who go home each day
    c) students enrolled in a religious school
    d) students who do not pay tuition

18. **possessed of**
    a) knowledgeable of
    b) motivated by
    c) desiring
    d) having

19. **funds**
    a) money
    b) supplies
    c) donors
    d) expenses

20. **gnawing**
    a) clawing persistently
    b) biting or chewing persistently
    c) grabbing or seizing persistently
    d) shoving or pushing persistently

The Nightly
Visitor

Chapter 10

Text
Pages
97-106

Perfect Score: 100   Score: _____

1. **to plague**
   a) to distract
   b) to frighten
   c) to torment
   d) to prevent

2. **vestments**
   a) golden chalice and ciborium
   b) altar linens used for the celebration
      of Mass
   c) valuable works of art
   d) garments worn by a priest when
      celebrating Mass

3. **huskiest**
   a holiest
   b) most intimidating
   c) boldest and bravest
   d) biggest and strongest

4. **din**
   a) loud, confused noise
   b) mysterious sound
   c) persistent clanging
   d) low-pitched sound

5. **lurch**
   a) explosion
   b) noise of an explosion
   c) abrupt tipping
   d) crashing sound

6. **hubbub**
   a) low-pitched sound
   b) uproar
   c) suffering
   d) annoying sound

7. **wrought-up**
   a terrified
   b) excited
   c) depressed
   d) crazy

8. **heaving**
   a) breaking
   b) rocking from side to side
   c) pushing and shoving
   d) rising and falling

9. **due**
   a) much
   b) agonizing
   c) careful
   d) sufficient

10. **scythe**
    a) tool used for cutting down trees
    b) tool used for planting trees
    c) tool used for cutting tall grass
    d) tool used for baling hay

11. **vessels**
    a) containers
    b) tools
    c) books
    d) statues

12. **descend upon**
    a) scare away
    b) close in on
    c) kill
    d) punish severely

13. **climax**
    a) the moment at which things return
       to normal
    b) the moment at which a problem is
       understood
    c) the strangest moment
    d) the most intense moment

14. **tumult**
    a) noisy commotion
    b) mysterious sound
    c) conflict, struggle
    d) war

15. on the threshold
a) in the center of a room
b) in the doorway
c) on the porch
d) on the front steps

16. bereft of
a) carried away by
b) not believing
c) deprived of
d) not using

17. anew
a) for the first time
b) immediately
c) again
d) for the second time

18. assume
a) take on
b) reject
c) take off
d) imagine

19. immense
a) extremely loud
b) nerve-racking
c) unusual
d) huge

20. taunt
a) test
b) trick
c) mock
d) argue with

The
Pastor

Chapter 11

Perfect Score: 100   **Score: _____**

1. scruple
a) question regarding one's vocation in life
b) error of a lax conscience
c) temptation to doubt the Faith
d) error of an overly strict conscience

2. welfare
a) health, well-being
b) holiness, sanctity
c) future
d) government

3. evident
a) understandable
b) helpful
c) obvious
d) distracting

4. resolutions
a) earnest intentions
b) desires
c) mutual agreements
d) regrets

5. dishonored
a treated with disrespect
b) treated with anger
c) treated with insincerity
d) behaved foolishly toward

6. worldly
a) wicked, malicious
b) recreational, relaxing
c) earthly, unreligious
d) enjoyable, pleasurable

7. canonized
a) martyred
b) declared a saint
c) beatified
d) sent to Rome for special service

8. laymen
a) persons who are not clerics
b) peasants
c) married persons
d) uneducated persons

9. **wistfully**
   a) longingly
   b) prayerfully
   c) peacefully
   d) impatiently

10. **resolutely**
   a) regretfully
   b) hesitantly
   c) definitely
   d) determinedly

11. **presently**
   a) in a little while, soon
   b) that same day
   c) without hesitation
   d) immediately

12. **fervent**
   a) pathetic
   b) ardent
   c) sincere
   d) desperate

13. **pulpit**
   a) platform used in preaching
   b) table in the sacristy
   c) table used in counseling
   d) kneeler

14. **enveloped**
   a) entered into
   b) affected deeply
   c) surrounded
   d) passed through

15. **unreservedly**
   a) despite obstacles, persistently
   b) without holding anything back
   c) without thinking
   d) prayerfully, devoutly

16. **foretaste**
   a) knowledge of something to come in the future
   b) prediction of something to come in the future
   c) the enjoyment of an experience
   d) a partial experience of something to come in the future

17. **merits**
   a) spiritual credits
   b) petitions, supplications
   c) blessings
   d) supernatural gifts

18. **admittance**
   a) approval
   b) permission to enter
   c) recognition of service
   d) schedule of payment

19. **headstrong**
   a) unpleasant
   b) unwise
   c) stubborn
   d) disobedient

20. **mildly**
   a) curiously
   b) gently
   c) sincerely
   d) thoughtfully

Miracles
In Ars

Chapter 12

Text
Pages
118-127

Perfect Score: 100　　　　　　　　　　　　　　**Score:** _____

1. **stifling**
   a) accepting
   b) ignoring
   c) suppressing
   d) preventing

2. **relic**
   a) teaching of a saint
   b) piece of the body of a saint
   c) picture or statue of a saint
   d) scapular

3. **rafters**
   a) wooden beams supporting the roof
   b) wooden beams supporting the floor
   c) wooden beams supporting the wall
   d) wooden beams used as floor boards

4. **a sprinkling**
   a) ten or fewer
   b) a large number of items that are
      small in size
   c) a small number of items scattered
      here and there
   d) five or fewer

5. **idlers**
   a) persons who are doing nothing
   b) persons who are gossiping
   c) persons who are causing trouble
   d) persons who are rude and selfish

6. **scoffers**
   a) persons who sit and listen
   b) persons who try to get in the way
   c) persons who watch and analyze
   d) persons who mock and ridicule

7. **invalids**
   a) persons who desire much attention
   b) persons who are sickly or disabled
   c) persons who suffer from a mental
      disorder
   d) persons with any urgent need

8. **ailment**
   a) problem or concern
   b) temptation
   c) bodily disorder
   d) sin or vice

9. **tuberculosis**
   a) a disease of the heart
   b) a disease of the lungs
   c) a disease of the stomach
   d) a disease of the bones

10. **circulate**
    a) cause problems
    b) be revealed
    c) be debated
    d) move around

11. **temporal**
    a) pertaining to eternal life
    b) pertaining to life on earth
    c) pertaining to the near future
    d) pertaining to the recent past

12. **materialized**
    a) were recorded
    b) were announced
    c) suddenly appeared
    d) vanished

13. showered
    a) given in abundance
    b) given as a reward
    c) given grudgingly
    d) given slowly

14. namesake
    a) a person named after another
    b) a person devoted to a certain saint
    c) feast day
    d) humble servant

15. cultivate
    a) create
    b) learn
    c) find
    d) nurture

16. flocked
    a) traveled
    b) went in a group
    c) walked
    d) came on the train

17. wrought
    a) discovered
    b) believed
    c) worked
    d) found

18. bestowed
    a) desired
    b) taken
    c) granted
    d) seen

19. persisted
    a) continued steadily
    b) spread steadily
    c) caused trouble
    d) became stronger

20. bewilderment
    a) surprise
    b) enjoyment
    c) suspense
    d) perplexity

Philomena
Makes Friends

Chapter 13

Text
Pages
128-138

Perfect Score: 100   Score: _____

1. clamoring
    a) questioning
    b) silently wondering
    c) raising an outcry
    d) doubting

2. publicity
    a) gossip
    b) annoyance
    c) admiration
    d) attention

3. secured
    a) obtained
    b) found
    c) received as a gift
    d) brought

4. intercession
    a) petitions on behalf of another
    b) petitions for oneself
    c) miracles
    d) healing power

5. assail
    a) abuse
    b) attack
    c) remind
    d) worry

6. prudently
    a) piously
    b) courageously
    c) wisely
    d) secretly

7. squarely
   a) quickly
   b) straightforwardly
   c) peacefully
   d) wisely

8. wayside
   a) rural
   b) remote
   c) far from the road
   d) close to the road

9. surmounted by
   a) having beside it
   b) having attached to it
   c) having on top of it
   d) having behind it

10. rustic
   a) plain and rough
   b) of old-fashioned design
   c) poorly constructed
   d) artistic

11. by dint of
   a) with great skill in
   b) by means of
   c) by sheer determination
   d) without the necessity of

12. briskly
   a) anxiously, in a stressed manner
   b) determinedly and purposefully
   c) quickly and energetically
   d) stubbornly, obstinately

13. burdens
   a) pains, sufferings
   b) heavy responsibilities
   c) rewards
   d) jobs, tasks

14. relishing
   a) thinking seriously about
   b) saying with admiration
   c) pleasurably appreciating
   d) meditating on

15. obliged
   a) persuaded
   b) disappointed
   c) discouraged
   d) required

16. calamity
   a) problem
   b) disaster
   c) serious event
   d) important event

17. Church Militant
   a) the saints in Heaven
   b) the souls in Purgatory
   c) Catholics on earth
   d) Catholics in the army

18. infirm
   a) suffering
   b) feeble
   c) mentally ill
   d) distressed

19. avail oneself of
   a) put up with
   b) flee from
   c) take advantage of
   d) discover

20. consecrated
   a) dedicated
   b) distinguished
   c) deserved
   d) decided

Perfect Score: 100   **Score:** _____

1. **stirring**
   a) starting to move
   b) stretching out
   c) enveloping
   d) moving back and forth

2. **commit oneself**
   a) openly state one's view
   b) have a positive attitude
   c) spread one's view
   d) have a negative attitude

3. **soaring**
   a) racing with great speed
   b) increasing in strength
   c) rising high
   d) growing to a great size

4. **brink**
   a) center
   b) bottom
   c) top
   d) edge

5. **devout**
   a) perfect
   b) serious
   c) pious
   d) peaceful

6. **Catacombs**
   a) ancient cathedrals of Rome
   b) lives of the early Christian saints
   c) great ages of Faith
   d) early Christian burial chambers

7. **compensated for**
   a) made up for
   b) gave comfort in
   c) gave proof of
   d) gave relief of

8. **remote**
   a) unheard-of
   b) distant
   c) mountainous
   d) barren

9. **solitude***
   a) mountaintop
   b) monastery
   c) lonely place
   d) desert island

10. **heed**
    a) respect
    b) attention
    c) stress
    d) logic

11. **soothingly**
    a) confidently
    b) sympathetically
    c) determinedly
    d) comfortingly

12. **solitude***
    a) quiet
    b) beauty
    c) aloneness
    d) peace

13. **tapestries**
    a) wall hangings
    b) leatherbound books
    c) vestments
    d) altar missals

14. **retire**
    a) go to sleep
    b) go to bed
    c) feel tired
    d) faint

* Note that this word can have different meanings depending on the context in which it is used.

15. **Breviary**
   a) book containing the Divine Office
   b) book containing the Gospels
   c) book containing the words of the Mass
   d) book containing the lives of the saints

16. **confided**
   a) bewailed
   b) expressed
   c) entrusted
   d) predicted

17. **wits**
   a) books and papers
   b) mental abilities
   c) hopes and desires
   d) sense of humor

18. **parcel**
   a) bag
   b) package
   c) knapsack
   d) suitcase

19. **exertion**
   a) experience
   b) excitement
   c) frustration
   d) effort

20. **haste**
   a) adventure
   b) hurry
   c) excitement
   d) disturbance

The Lost Week	**Chapter 15**	Text Pages 149-158

Perfect Score: 100   Score: _____

1. **trudged**
   a) walked steadily
   b) walked tirelessly
   c) walked laboriously or wearily
   d) walked slowly and carefully

2. **lapsed**
   a) slipped gradually
   b) were inclined
   c) returned
   d) became accustomed

3. **protested**
   a) said
   b) demonstrated
   c) objected
   d) suggested

4. **forsaken**
   a) forgotten
   b) abandoned
   c) ignored
   d) followed

5. **deserted**
   a) in disrepair
   b) overgrown with brush
   c) damaged or destroyed
   d) empty, abandoned

6. **pilgrims**
   a) persons on a religious trip
   b) persons on a business trip
   c) persons on a pleasure trip
   d) persons on any type of trip

7. **distressing**
   a) causing amazement
   b) causing pain or sorrow
   c) causing anger
   d) causing change for the better

8. **disclose**
   a) distance oneself from
   b) publicize
   c) reveal
   d) discuss

9. **whereabouts**
   a) the place where a person or thing will be
   b) the place where a person or thing was last seen
   c) the place where a person or thing usually is
   d) the place where a person or thing is

10. **grimly**
    a) angrily, heatedly
    b) apathetically, uncaringly
    c) seriously, sternly
    d) eagerly, enthusiastically

11. **despatched**
    a) sent
    b) entrusted
    c) assigned
    d) released

12. **at everyone's beck and call**
    a) subject to every request
    b) talked or gossiped about by all
    c) summoning people from everywhere
    d) giving orders to everyone

13. **shirking**
    a) rebelling against
    b) avoiding, evading
    c) confronting
    d) de-emphasizing

14. **bade farewell**
    a) looked at sadly
    b) gave a greeting
    c) said goodbye
    d) gave a blessing

15. **age-old**
    a) holy
    b) powerful
    c) forgotten
    d) ancient

16. **sanctify**
    a) inspire
    b) make holy
    c) give assistance
    d) influence toward good

17. **embraced**
    a) clasped another in one's arms
    b) gave a formal salute
    c) blessed
    d) shook another's hand

18. **landscape**
    a) forests
    b) fields
    c) greenery
    d) scenery

19. **prolonging**
    a) fixing
    b) extending
    c) creating
    d) delaying

20. **start**
    a) sudden movement
    b) sharp pain
    c) stumble
    d) cry of pain

The
Return

Chapter 16

Text
Pages
159-170

Perfect Score: 100   Score: _____

1. **procured**
   a) obtained
   b) sent off
   c) set aside
   d) requested

2. **desolate**
   a) scenic, picturesque
   b) quiet, peaceful
   c) beautiful
   d) lonely, deserted

3. **objected**
   a) attempted to persuade
   b) stated in protest
   c) stated bitterly
   d) pointed out

4. **dismissed**
   a) dismantled
   b) sent away
   c) abandoned
   d) paid for

5. **hermit**
   a) person who lives in a small town
   b) person who lives among monks
   c) person who lives alone
   d) person who lives a religious life

6. **plodded**
   a) walked with determination
   b) walked carefully
   c) walked thoughtfully
   d) walked slowly, heavily

7. **stammered**
   a) said haltingly
   b) called out
   c) announced
   d) said with enthusiasm

8. **grudge**
   a) feeling of abandonment
   b) feeling of sorrow
   c) feeling of resentment
   d) feeling of confusion

9. **pealing**
   a) low-pitched ringing
   b) sweet tinkling
   c) playing of hymns
   d) loud ringing

10. **litany**
    a) a kind of repetitive prayer
    b) a kind of hymn
    c) a kind of sermon
    d) a procession

11. **besieged with**
    a) made anxious by
    b) fatigued, exhausted by
    c) followed by
    d) pressed, surrounded by

12. **throngs**
    a) groups of pilgrims
    b) large crowds
    c) travelers
    d) crowds of impatient people

13. **conceal**
    a) lie
    b) fear
    c) hide
    d) pretend

14. **detestable**
    a) ugly
    b) dangerous
    c) outrageous
    d) hateful

15. instrument
   a) end
   b) schedule
   c) tool
   d) program

16. reflection
   a) hesitation
   b) thought
   c) prudence
   d) delay

17. relented
   a) made a decision
   b) gave in
   c) resolved
   d) forgave

18. launched into (figurative meaning)
   a) began energetically
   b) eased into, slipped into
   c) continued with
   d) ended with

19. attentively
   a) anxiously
   b) enthusiatically
   c) hesitantly
   d) carefully

20. numbness
   a) the state of being filled with worry
   b) the state of being unable to feel
   c) the state of feeling hopeless
   d) the state of having one's feelings hurt

Changes In Ars	# Chapter 17	Text Pages 171-180

Perfect Score: 100   Score: _____

1. foundation
   a) basis, grounding
   b) end result
   c) bank account
   d) procedure, method

2. laywomen
   a) women who teach catechism
   b) women who sing in the choir
   c) women who do not hold positions of authority
   d) women who are not religious sisters

3. manifested
   a) discovered
   b) obeyed
   c) planned
   d) made known

4. resigned
   a) accepting
   b) joyful
   c) reluctant
   d) enthusiastic

5. comparatively
   a) seemingly
   b) relatively
   c) almost
   d) definitely

6. respectively
   a) respectfully
   b) in perspective
   c) in the order stated
   d) in the way things have been arranged

7. **quarters**
   a) bedrooms
   b) places where people work
   c) places where people live
   d) places where people study

8. **relinquish**
   a) forget about
   b) give up
   c) deny
   d) exercise

9. **afflicted**
   a) affected
   b) established
   c) troubled
   d) instituted

10. **inaugurate**
    a) begin officially
    b) plan thoroughly
    c) suggest tactfully
    d) speak about

11. **mission**
    a) series of sermons and church
       services to renew the spiritual life
       of Catholics
    b) series of catechism classes for
       children
    c) series of instructions for the
       conversion of non-Catholics
    d) series of parish fund-raising
       activities

12. **practical**
    a) theoretically sound
    b) workable
    c) beneficial
    d) popular

13. **franc**
    a) unit of money used all over Europe
    b) unit of money used in France
    c) unit of money used in France, Spain
       and Italy
    d) unit of money used all over northern
       Europe

14. **defray**
    a) extend
    b) profit by
    c) exceed
    d) pay

15. **peddling**
    a) going from place to place loaning
       things
    b) going from place to place seeking
       something
    c) going from place to place selling
       goods
    d) going from place to place giving
       things away

16. **miser**
    a) one who lives poorly in order
       to accumulate money
    b) one who steals in order to
       accumulate money
    c) one who spends money on grand
       projects
    d) one who sells goods to his friends

17. **ermine**
    a) green gemstones
    b) white fur
    c) purple fabric
    d) gold

18. **proceedings**
    a) celebrations
    b) perplexities
    c) events
    d) disappointments

19. **recollection**
    a) mortification and penance
    b) works of charity
    c) manual labor
    d) prayerful silence

20. **perpetual**
    a) virtuous
    b) according to the Rule
    c) continual, continuing always
    d) lasting from sunrise to sunset

A Third
Flight

Chapter 18

Text
Pages
181-191

Perfect Score: 100   **Score: _____**

1. **curate**
   a) priest who assists the bishop at the cathedral
   b) priest who offers Mass but may not hear Confessions
   c) assistant priest in a parish
   d) priest who teaches at a seminary

2. **transferred**
   a) fired
   b) promoted
   c) replaced
   d) moved

3. **residence**
   a) familiarity, acquaintance
   b) long visit
   c) doing a good job
   d) period of living in a specific place

4. **officiated at**
   a) performed a ceremony
   b) attended a ceremony
   c) appeared
   d) prayed

5. **radiant** (literal meaning)
   a) warm
   b) red
   c) shining
   d) pale

6. **spell**
   a) exhibition
   b) period of bodily disorder
   c) cause of something
   d) result of something

7. **vigorously**
   a) acceptingly
   b) hurriedly
   c) frustratedly
   d) energetically

8. **provisions**
   a) food to be bought
   b) food to be sold
   c) a supply of food
   d) good food

9. **bitterness**
   a) sharpness, severity
   b) fatigue, weariness
   c) perplexity, bewilderment
   d) discouragement, depression

10. **likewise**
    a) for the same reason
    b) even more so
    c) in the same way
    d) following someone else's example

11. **Angelus**
    a) bells announcing the time for a devotion honoring the Passion
    b) bells announcing the time for a devotion honoring the Annunciation
    c) bells announcing the time for a devotion honoring the Presentation
    d) bells announcing the time for a devotion honoring the Ascension

12. **restraining**
    a) holding back
    b) holding over
    c) holding out
    d) holding under

13. **severe**
    a) stern
    b) squinting
    c) annoyed
    d) intense

THE CURÉ OF ARS

14. dirge
   a) cheerful, slow tune
   b) high-pitched, slow tune
   c) mournful, slow tune
   d) tune

15. cobbler
   a) one who makes hats
   b) one who makes tools
   c) one who bakes desserts
   d) one who makes shoes

16. surveying
   a) viewing
   b) committing to memory
   c) grieving over
   d) pondering over

17. tumultuous
   a) shocking
   b) dangerous
   c) disastrous
   d) disorderly

18. massing
   a) gathering in a large group
   b) becoming rowdy
   c) separating into small groups
   d) threatening

19. amidst (amid)
   a) beside
   b) surrounded by
   c) joined with
   d) near

20. pity
   a) piety
   b) fear
   c) compassion
   d) hope

The Work
Continues

Chapter 19

Text
Pages
192-202

Perfect Score: 100   Score: _____

1. sacristy
   a) room in which priests pray the Divine Office
   b) room in which Mass is offered
   c) room in which sacred vessels and vestments are kept
   d) room in which religion classes are held

2. surged
   a) moved forward slowly
   b) moved in a chaotic manner
   c) pushed and shoved forward
   d) moved forward like a wave

3. incredulously
   a) unbelievingly
   b) joyfully
   c) selfishly
   d) exhaustedly

4. secluded
   a) secure
   b) private
   c) distant
   d) quiet

5. **attain**
   a) attempt
   b) achieve
   c) discover
   d) receive

6. **persevere**
   a) begin despite possible obstacles
   b) stop because of obstacles
   c) continue despite obstacles
   d) be perfect

7. **Third Order members** (tertiaries)
   a) priests who belong to a religious order
   b) religious brothers in a religious order
   c) nuns in a religious order
   d) lay members of a religious order

8. **rendered**
   a) obtained, acquired
   b) renewed, restored
   c) given, done
   d) requested, asked

9. **distinguished**
   a) worthwhile
   b) outstanding
   c) public
   d) political

10. **imperial**
    a) having to do with an emperor
    b) having to do with a king
    c) having to do with the military
    d) having to do with the clergy

11. **putting stock in**
    a) having respect for
    b) having confidence in
    c) understanding, comprehending
    d) refusing to believe

12. **charge**
    a) someone who is in trouble or who needs special care
    b) young person attending school
    c) someone committed to one's care
    d) someone who is sick or injured

13. **restoration**
    a) requirement
    b) improvement, betterment
    c) returning to a former good condition
    d) unexpected gift

14. **catechist**
    a) teacher of basic religious truths
    b) professor of theology
    c) seminary instructor
    d) doctor who visits the sick in their homes

15. **Veni Creator**
    a) a prayer to the Blessed Virgin Mary
    b) a prayer to the Sacred Heart of Jesus
    c) a prayer to the Precious Blood of Jesus
    d) a prayer to the Holy Spirit

16. **patroness**
    a) man who founded
    b) woman who founded
    c) special heavenly helper (male)
    d) special heavenly helper (female)

17. **foster**
    a) promote and encourage
    b) lay a foundation for
    c) teach and explain
    d) demonstrate

18. **professed**
    a) boasted
    b) promised
    c) pretended
    d) stated

19. **impelled**
    a) enlightened
    b) urged
    c) excited
    d) enthused

20. **stimulating**
    a) sanctifying
    b) consoling, removing sorrow
    c) rousing to action
    d) giving security

The End of
The Road

Chapter 20

Text
Pages
203-211

Perfect Score: 100   Score: _____

1. **oppressive**
   a) burdensome
   b) immense
   c) supportive
   d) painful

2. **ebbing**
   a) returning
   b) changing
   c) increasing
   d) declining

3. **the Holy Sacrifice**
   a) the Divine Office
   b) the Mass
   c) the seven Sacraments
   d) one's daily duties

4. **Extreme Unction**
   a) Last Anointing
   b) Holy Viaticum
   c) pontifical blessing
   d) absolution

5. **scarcely**
   a) certainly not
   b) fearfully
   c) probably not
   d) barely

6. **novena**
   a) a devotion or prayer prayed for
      seven days to obtain a special
      favor
   b) a devotion or prayer prayed for
      seventeen days to obtain a special
      favor
   c) a devotion or prayer prayed for
      nine days to obtain a special
      favor
   d) a devotion or prayer prayed for
      twelve days to obtain a special
      favor

7. **feeble**
   a) confident
   b) slow
   c) weak
   d) hopeless

8. **abating**
   a) intensifying
   b) lessening
   c) improving
   d) cooling

9. **heedless of**
   a) distracted by
   b) suffering from
   c) careful of
   d) unmindful of

10. **intercede**
    a) bless with a relic
    b) perform a miracle
    c) ask on behalf of another
    d) ask on behalf of oneself

11. **choicest**
    a) good
    b) desirable
    c) pleasing
    d) best

12. **Last Rites**
    a) last will and testament
    b) Extreme Unction and Holy
       Viaticum
    c) Holy Communion and Holy Viaticum
    d) Holy Orders

13. **toll**
    a) sound
    b) sound with high-pitched tones
    c) sound with quick, repetitive strokes
    d) sound with slow, measured
       strokes

14. reflecting
    a) deciding
    b) pondering
    c) demonstrating
    d) regretting

15. mournful
    a) expressing sorrow
    b) expressing peace
    c) expressing devotion
    d) expressing respect

16. ominous
    a) expressing sorrow
    b) emitting a muffled sound
    c) foreboding
    d) loud

17. lashed
    a) struck as with a whip
    b) struck as with a fist
    c) broke noisily
    d) dribbled down

18. conduct
    a) encourage
    b) reward
    c) inspire
    d) lead

19. Jerusalem (figurative meaning)
    a) Judgment
    b) sainthood
    c) Purgatory
    d) Heaven

20. yoke (literal meaning)
    a) stool used to reach high objects
    b) tool used for constructing buildings
    c) device used for carrying a load
    d) device used for cultivating crops

Instructions: Circle the letter of the answer which best matches the meaning of the vocabulary word.

| The Baby of the Martin Family | **Chapter 1** | Text Pages 1-10 |

Perfect Score: 100   Score: _____

1. **vocation**
   a) calling
   b) idea
   c) plan
   d) devotion

2. **cloister**
   a) convent or monastery
   b) enclosed convent or monastery
   c) cave where hermits live
   d) rectory where priests live

3. **consecrated to**
   a) blessed by
   b) prayed for
   c) named after
   d) dedicated to

4. **alas**
   a) surprisingly
   b) unfortunately
   c) happily
   d) fortunately

5. **afflicted**
   a) inconvenienced
   b) inspired
   c) astonished
   d) distressed

6. **prospering**
   a) becoming up-to-date
   b) becoming successful
   c) becoming popular
   d) becoming famous

7. **marveled at**
   a) was envious of
   b) accepted
   c) was astonished at
   d) enjoyed

8. **trials**
   a) troubles, difficulties
   b) merits, virtues
   c) unexpected events
   d) interesting experiences

9. **presently**
   a) in a little while, soon
   b) after a few years
   c) a long time ago
   d) later

10. **godmother**
    a) woman or girl after whom a child is named at Baptism
    b) woman or girl who sponsors a child at Baptism
    c) older sister of a child who is baptized
    d) woman or girl who helps raise a child

11. **procession**
    a) a group of persons walking
    b) a line of persons walking
    c) a family walking
    d) a crowd of persons walking

12. **heartily**
    a) teasingly
    b) politely, in a well-mannered way
    c) without restraint, vigorously
    d) humorously

13. **parted**
    a) forgotten
    b) neglected
    c) substituted
    d) separated

14. **humanity**
    a) mankind
    b) childhood
    c) family
    d) babyhood

15. **pale**
    a) ill
    b) weak
    c) dull
    d) colorless

16. **mite**
    a) very sickly creature
    b) very small creature
    c) very pale creature
    d) very delicate creature

17. **fervent**
    a) ardent, intense
    b) persistent, persevering
    c) long and thorough
    d) sincere, genuine

18. **on the contrary**
    a) similarly
    b) as expected
    c) just the opposite
    d) very stubbornly

19. **contented**
    a) safe
    b) peaceful
    c) friendly
    d) satisfied

20. **remarked**
    a) protested
    b) commented
    c) hinted
    d) announced

Chapter 2

Text Pages 11-20

Perfect Score: 100

Score: _____

1. **permanently**
    a) lasting indefinitely
    b) lasting for a short while
    c) periodically
    d) lasting for a long time

2. **boarding school**
    a) school where students learn religion
    b) school where students receive meals and lodging
    c) school that prepares students for the religious life
    d) school where students work to pay for classes

VOCABULARY QUIZ WORKBOOK

3. amused
a) puzzled
b) satisfied
c) impressed
d) entertained

4. employed
a) volunteered
b) persuaded
c) hired
d) implored

5. intervals
a) spaces of time
b) weekdays
c) drop-off points
d) workrooms

6. heights
a) depths
b) levels
c) understanding
d) feeling

7. solemn
a) injured
b) serious
c) miserable
d) abandoned

8. grieving
a) disobeying
b) causing anger
c) offending
d) causing sorrow

9. reproachfully
a) disapprovingly
b) informatively
c) disgustedly
d) wisely

10. cross
a) violent
b) deceitful
c) bad-tempered
d) proud

11. deceit
a) unkind act
b) decisive act
c) selfish act
d) dishonest act

12. alter
a) make up for
b) hide
c) change
d) answer

13. air
a) manner
b) breath
c) word
d) gesture

14. intention
a) sacrifice offered up
b) virtue practiced
c) blessing requested
d) suffering endured

15. accompany
a) assist
b) lead
c) go along with
d) follow

16. shrine
a) place devoted to health and healing
b) place devoted to helping foreign visitors
c) place of research and study
d) place devoted to God or a saint

17. earnestly
a) affectionately, sweetly
b) sincerely, intently
c) reassuringly, comforting
d) honestly, truthfully

18. affectionate
a) understanding
b) loving
c) good-natured
d) cheerful

19. in vain
  a) useless
  b) unimportant
  c) too difficult
  d) insincere

20. awaited
  a) was endured by
  b) was in store for
  c) made up for
  d) made use of

Learning to Live Without
Our Dear Mama

Chapter 3

Perfect Score: 100   Score: _____

1. exiles
  a) imprisoned persons
  b) hermits
  c) orphans
  d) banished persons

2. bitterly
  a) with deep suffering
  b) without hope
  c) with many tears
  d) with loud wailing

3. unburden oneself
  a) make progress
  b) obtain relief
  c) obtain knowledge
  d) obtain joy

4. murmured
  a) said loudly
  b) announced
  c) suggested
  d) said softly

5. advanced
  a) moved
  b) moved away
  c) moved forward
  d) moved around

6. caress
  a) stroke affectionately
  b) pat on the back
  c) pat on the head
  d) embrace

7. due
  a) much
  b) careful
  c) adequate
  d) lengthy

8. purchased
  a) bargained for
  b) decided upon
  c) bought
  d) rented

9. estate
  a) large piece of forested land
  b) property belonging to a famous person
  c) large house
  d) large piece of property with a large house on it

10. institution
  a) educational or charitable establishment
  b) government organization
  c) Catholic organization
  d) money-making business

11. sanctuary
  a) the part of a church where the priests vest
  b) the part of a church where the high altar stands
  c) the part of a church where the baptismal font stands
  d) the part of a church where the choir sits

VOCABULARY QUIZ WORKBOOK

12. **grating**
   a) a fixed frame of bars to exclude persons
   b) an iron gate to exclude persons
   c) a metal door to exclude persons
   d) a heavy wall to exclude persons

13. **angling**
   a) fishing with a net
   b) fishing with a hook and line
   c) walking in the country
   d) shopping at open-air markets

14. **excursions**
   a) drives
   b) outings
   c) adventures
   d) walks

15. **flattered**
   a) surprised
   b) complimented
   c) embarrassed
   d) shy

16. **bass**
   a) high in pitch
   b) soothing
   c) low in pitch
   d) musical

17. **tyrant**
   a) emperor
   b) oppressive ruler
   c) pirate
   d) army general

18. **customary**
   a) anticipated
   b) usual
   c) prudent
   d) expected

19. **Purgatory**
   a) place where souls undergo temporary punishment
   b) place where souls undergo everlasting punishment
   c) place where souls of unbaptized infants go
   d) place where souls are tested for their worthiness of Heaven

20. **the blessed**
   a) the saints in Heaven
   b) the saints in Heaven and saintly persons on earth
   c) famous saints
   d) canonized saints

A Mysterious Illness	**Chapter 4**	Text Pages 32-40

Perfect Score: 100   Score: _____

1. **seized**
   a) passed over
   b) bothered
   c) took hold of
   d) surprised

2. **indignant**
   a) regretful and sorry
   b) insulted and angry
   c) indifferent and unconcerned
   d) tired and exhausted

3. **avail**
   a) use or advantage
   b) good fortune
   c) relief or consolation
   d) sincere effort

4. **plagued**
   a) frightened
   b) tormented
   c) bored
   d) disgusted

5. taunts
   a) cruel practical jokes
   b) competition, rivalry
   c) mockery, ridicule
   d) underhanded behavior

6. splendidly
   a) scholastically
   b) skillfully
   c) magnificently
   d) sufficiently

7. sensitive
   a) easily persuaded
   b) understanding
   c) scholastically superior
   d) easily hurt

8. hermit
   a) person who lives in solitude
   b) person who lives in a monastery or convent
   c) person who lives a holy life in the midst of the world
   d) person with limited eyesight

9. model (adjective)
   a) honorable
   b) respectable
   c) holy
   d) ideal

10. calamity
   a) disaster
   b) adventure
   c) accident
   d) mistake

11. venture
   a) take the time
   b) take the risk
   c) ask permission
   d) realize the need

12. parlor
   a) visiting room
   b) dining room
   c) lobby
   d) front porch

13. strain
   a) stress
   b) excitement
   c) disappointment
   d) sadness

14. departure
   a) act of changing
   b) act of moving
   c) act of arriving
   d) act of leaving

15. tell (on)
   a) bring illness to
   b) show its effect on
   c) make up for
   d) make way for

16. promptly
   a) successfully
   b) with good will
   c) right away
   d) dutifully

17. novena
   a) devotion lasting 7 days
   b) devotion lasting 9 days
   c) devotion lasting 12 days
   d) devotion lasting 30 days

18. imploring
   a) begging
   b) grieving
   c) meditating
   d) worrying

19. storming (Heaven)
   a) obeying with humility
   b) listening to with attention
   c) struggling against despair
   d) besieging with pleas

20. radiant
   a) shining
   b) gorgeous
   c) lovely
   d) lively

My First Holy
Communion

Chapter 5

Text
Pages
41-51

Perfect Score: 100   Score: _____

1. **reluctant**
   a) stubbornly refusing
   b) hesitant or unwilling
   c) unprepared, not ready
   d) no longer able

2. **scruples**
   a) sorrows, griefs
   b) regrets
   c) complaints
   d) anxieties, doubts

3. **obstinate**
   a) stubborn
   b) selfish
   c) childish
   d) oversensitive

4. **meditation**
   a) mental prayer
   b) vocal prayer
   c) sacrifice
   d) eternal life

5. **preceding**
   a) following
   b) simultaneous with
   c) previous to
   d) later than

6. **retreat**
   a) brief withdrawal from the world
      for a spiritual purpose
   b) visit to a convent or monastery
   c) preparation for an important
      spiritual event
   d) period of reading and study

7. **banish**
   a) destroy
   b) drive away
   c) prevent
   d) forbid

8. **apparently**
   a) unfortunately
   b) predictably
   c) evidently
   d) undoubtedly

9. **liberty**
   a) freedom
   b) privilege
   c) authority
   d) boldness

10. **vast**
    a) impressive
    b) intense
    c) immense
    d) everlasting

11. **consecration to**
    a) special reparation to
    b) special dedication to
    c) special petition to
    d) special thanksgiving to

12. **resolutions**
    a) obligations, duties
    b) desires, wishes
    c) expectations, anticipations
    d) intentions, determinations

13. **Memorare**
    a) a prayer of thanksgiving to Our Lord
    b) a prayer of petition to Our Lord
    c) a prayer of thanksgiving to Our
       Lady
    d) a prayer of petition to Our Lady

14. **counsel**
    a) supernatural prudence
    b) supernatural penitence
    c) supernatural perseverance
    d) supernatural patience

15. fortitude
   a) supernatural wisdom
   b) supernatural faith
   c) supernatural knowledge
   d) supernatural courage

16. amid
   a) surrounding
   b) with
   c) surrounded by
   d) including

17. enrolled
   a) trained
   b) educated
   c) initiated
   d) registered

18. sodality
   a) association of seamstresses
   b) scholastic association
   c) association of future nuns
   d) pious association

19. pronounced
   a) distinct, obvious
   b) disturbing, aggravating
   c) perfect, ideal
   d) effective, useful

20. self-consciousness
   a) confidence in one's own worth or
      abilities
   b) feeling of being ill at ease with others
   c) difficulty in getting along with others
   d) frustration over small problems in
      daily life

My First Child
Of Grace

Chapter 6

Text
Pages
52-62

Perfect Score: 100   Score: _____

1. conversion
   a) transformation
   b) acceptance
   c) realization
   d) exchange

2. longed
   a) made plans
   b) desired ardently
   c) loved
   d) began

3. noted
   a) accepted
   b) were pleased at
   c) expected
   d) observed

4. arose
   a) achieved
   b) came up
   c) was announced
   d) was figured out

5. pagans
   a) those who live immoral lives
   b) those who have left the True Church
   c) those who do not know the true God
   d) those who claim that there is no God

6. persisted
   a) insisted
   b) pertained
   c) continued steadily
   d) took root

7. **feast**
    a) day of fasting and penance
    b) day of holy celebration
    c) day of obligatory Mass attendance
    d) day of religious procession

8. **Pentecost**
    a) day commemorating Our Lady's visitation to St. Elizabeth
    b) day commemorating the descent of the Holy Ghost upon the Apostles
    c) day commemorating the Angel's announcement to Our Lady of Christ's Incarnation
    d) day commemorating the Presentation of Jesus in the Temple

9. **Vespers**
    a) morning prayers of the Divine Office
    b) mid-day prayers of the Divine Office
    c) evening prayers of the Divine Office
    d) midnight prayers of the Divine Office

10. **consent**
    a) permission
    b) response
    c) help
    d) opinion

11. **cherished**
    a) secret
    b) special
    c) sacred
    d) beloved

12. **canon**
    a) priest who is pastor of a parish
    b) priest who assists the pastor of a parish
    c) priest who is a member of a religious order
    d) priest who works at a cathedral

13. **affairs**
    a) communications with the outside world
    b) vocational questions
    c) concerns, business
    d) problems, difficulties

14. **prioress**
    a) priest who governs a monastery of monks
    b) nun who governs an enclosed convent of nuns
    c) nun who speaks with visitors to the convent
    d) nun who entered the convent first

15. **state**
    a) win
    b) publicize
    c) mention
    d) declare

16. **remorse**
    a) admission of wrongdoing
    b) satisfaction at wrongdoing
    c) regret for wrongdoing
    d) change from wrongdoing

17. **blasphemed**
    a) insulted God or holy things
    b) ignored God or holy things
    c) spoke with pride
    d) spoke with anger

18. **gratitude**
    a) joy
    b) excitement
    c) thankfulness
    d) grace

19. timidly
    a) in a manner showing respect
    b) in a manner showing lack of self-confidence
    c) in a manner showing dignity
    d) in a manner showing lack of self-consciousness

20. pilgrimage
    a) study for a religious purpose
    b) meeting for a religious purpose
    c) journey for a religious purpose
    d) purchase for a religious purpose

Disappointment
In Rome

Chapter 7

Text
Pages
63-74

Perfect Score: 100

Score: _____

1. prospect
    a) program
    b) schedule
    c) decision
    d) anticipation

2. restored
    a) returned to previous condition
    b) improved the condition of
    c) saved from destruction
    d) helped, assisted

3. proceeded
    a) continued on
    b) preceded
    c) superseded
    d) interceded

4. picturesque
    a) antiquated, old-fashioned
    b) scenic
    c) mountainous or hilly
    d) Swiss

5. climax
    a) anticipation
    b) low point
    c) high point
    d) reason

6. vicar
    a) person who is a substitute or agent for someone else
    b) person who holds the highest position in an organization
    c) person who serves as a model for others
    d) person who continues the work of someone who has left

7. the Eternal City
    a) the Coliseum
    b) Rome
    c) Paris
    d) Venice

8. excavations
    a) hiding places formed by digging
    b) large holes formed by digging
    c) construction sites
    d) historical sites examined by digging

9. gaping
    a) dark and deep
    b) dangerous
    c) having rounded edges
    d) wide open

10. martyrdom
    a) death of any saint
    b) death in Rome
    c) death for Christ
    d) death of an early Christian

11. barricade
a) wall
b) barrier
c) fence
d) gate

12. catacombs
a) underground burial chambers of the ancient Israelites
b) underground burial chambers of the Apostles
c) underground burial chambers of the early Popes
d) underground burial chambers of the early Christians

13. venerated
a) viewed, gazed at
b) carried in procession
c) revered, honored
d) petitioned, supplicated

14. fragments
a) images
b) small pieces
c) relics
d) pieces of wood

15. reliquary
a) special section of a church or chapel
b) container for relics
c) rosary case
d) case for nails or wood

16. torrents
a) lightning and thunder
b) storm
c) violent downpour
d) steady mist

17. presume
a) decide
b) consider
c) dare
d) attempt

18. verdict
a) solution
b) judgment
c) information
d) reason

19. heedless
a) ignorant
b) disdainful
c) uncomprehending
d) unmindful

20. curt
a) commanding
b) abrupt
c) threatening
d) discreet

Carmel
At Last

Chapter 8

Text
Pages
75-85

Perfect Score: 100   Score: _____

1. glory
a) meditate
b) exult
c) glorify
d) enjoy

2. postulant
a) person considering entering religious life
b) person trying out religious life
c) person who has received the religious habit
d) novice preparing for religious profession

3. a religious
   a) a priest
   b) an unmarried Catholic
   c) a member of a religious order
   d) any spiritual person

4. content
   a) excite
   b) relieve
   c) consume
   d) satisfy

5. prevailed
   a) occurred
   b) weakened
   c) predominated
   d) strengthened

6. assisted at (Mass)
   a) attended and participated in
       spiritually
   b) served at the altar
   c) attended, sitting in special seats in
       the front of the church
   d) celebrated

7. agony
   a) finality
   b) effort
   c) intense emotion of any kind
   d) intense suffering

8. threshold
   a) grating
   b) floor of a doorway
   c) side of the sanctuary
   d) vestibule of a church

9. respectively
   a) with great respect
   b) with great precision
   c) in that order
   d) in that way

10. surveyed
   a) counted
   b) nodded respectfully to
   c) looked around at
   d) gazed at intently

11. Te Deum
   a) prayer of praise and thanksgiving
   b) prayer of penance and mortification
   c) a prayer prayed only in monasteries
   d) *Pater Noster*

12. delegate
   a) messenger
   b) representative
   c) superior
   d) assistant

13. quick (literal meaning)
   a) painfully sensitive flesh beneath
       the fingernails
   b) painfully sensitive flesh between the
       toes
   c) painfully sensitive flesh on the
       fingertips
   d) painfully sensitive flesh around the
       eyes

14. chanting
   a) singing by an all-female choir
   b) singing in elaborate harmonies
   c) singing in a high-pitched voice
   d) singing in simple, repetitive melodies

15. Divine Office
   a) official prayers said at various
       times throughout the day
   b) official prayers said before and after
       Mass
   c) official prayers to certain saints
   d) official prayers said after Lent

16. cell
   a) choir stall
   b) church pew
   c) place at table
   d) small room

17. exclusive
   a) unnecessary
   b) selfish, greedy
   c) not shared, individual
   d) unlimited, free of restraint

18. confine
a) guide
b) limit
c) command
d) control

19. moderate
a) clarify
b) restrain
c) enliven
d) purify

20. garb
a) ugly clothing
b) worldly clothing
c) clothing
d) old clothing

<table>
<tr><td>Precious
Crosses</td><td># Chapter 9</td><td>Text
Pages
86-97</td></tr>
</table>

Perfect Score: 100   Score: _____

1. mild
a) not unnoticed
b) not unintended
c) not severe
d) not permanent

2. paralysis
a) injury to a body part
b) loss of movement
c) disease in a body part
d) loss of memory

3. bewilderment
a) great fear
b) great joy
c) intense concern
d) great puzzlement

4. pondered
a) worried greatly
b) thought deeply
c) daydreamed
d) grieved deeply

5. revelation
a) deep spirituality
b) meditation
c) something made known
d) something that puzzles

6. confirmed
a) shown to be true
b) shown to be false
c) shown to be virtuous
d) shown to be not virtuous

7. in religion
a) in the religious life
b) after Baptism
c) prayerfully
d) as a Catholic

8. Clothing Day
a) day on which one becomes a postulant
b) day on which one becomes a novice
c) day on which one makes one's religious profession
d) day on which one does laundry in a convent

9. tulle
a) a woolen fabric
b) a linen fabric
c) a white fabric
d) a sheer fabric

10. **without reserve**
    a) prayerfully
    b) completely
    c) solemnly
    d) tearfully

11. **victim**
    a) one who makes up for one's own sins
    b) one who suffers on behalf of others
    c) one who suffers from any cause
    d) one who prays for sinners

12. **strains**
    a) hymns
    b) voices
    c) melodies
    d) instruments

13. **charge**
    a) privilege
    b) counsel
    c) responsibility
    d) routine

14. **novice**
    a) one who is considering entering
       a monastery
    b) one who is trying out the religious
       life
    c) one who has received the religious
       habit and is preparing for
       religious profession
    d) one who has made religious
       profession

15. **refectory**
    a) convent parlor
    b) convent recreation room
    c) convent corridor
    d) convent dining room

16. **rheumatism**
    a) disorder characterized by heart
       pains
    b) disorder characterized by violent
       mood swings
    c) disorder characterized by pain
       in the joints or muscles
    d) disorder characterized by memory
       loss

17. **raiment**
    a) cloak
    b) radiance
    c) uniform
    d) clothing

18. **adorned**
    a) decorated
    b) simplified
    c) changed
    d) improved

19. **henceforth**
    a) in the future
    b) soon
    c) in a little while
    d) from now on

20. **chastity**
    a) humility
    b) charity
    c) faith
    d) purity

Life in the
Convent

Chapter 10

Text
Pages
98-107

Perfect Score: 100   **Score:** _____

1. **weary** (months)
   a) tiresome
   b) unending
   c) difficult
   d) challenging

2. **labor**
   a) pray
   b) prepare
   c) work
   d) learn

3. **religious profession**
   a) ceremony of receiving the religious
      habit
   b) ceremony of becoming a novice
   c) ceremony of making the vows of
      religious life
   d) any ceremony in church

4. **eve**
   a) day of
   b) day before
   c) day after
   d) day one week before

5. **assembled**
   a) prepared
   b) gathered
   c) entered
   d) hurried

6. **Matins**
   a) morning prayer of the Divine Office
   b) mid-day prayer of the Divine Office
   c) mid-afternoon prayer of the Divine
      Office
   d) evening prayer of the Divine Office

7. **prostrate**
   a) stretched out face down
   b) curled up
   c) on one's side
   d) flat on one's back

8. **duly**
   a) without restraint
   b) truly, sincerely
   c) without regret
   d) properly, sufficiently

9. **captive**
   a) soul
   b) inhabitant
   c) sufferer
   d) prisoner

10. **unhindered**
    a) not held out
    b) not held over
    c) not held back
    d) not held

11. **obstacle**
    a) object
    b) obstruction
    c) being
    d) evil

12. **ecstasies**
    a) earthly possessions
    b) honors, privileges
    c) family affections
    d) rapturous joys

13. **orderly**
    a) devout, pious
    b) following regular patterns
    c) commanded by superiors
    d) laborious

14. indifferent
  a) sinful
  b) uncaring
  c) corrupted
  d) ignorant

15. malady
  a) epidemic, plague
  b) injury or wound
  c) disease or disorder
  d) suffering, pain

16. retained
  a) received
  b) enjoyed
  c) asked for
  d) kept

17. heed
  a) favor
  b) attention
  c) gratitude
  d) trust

18. severity
  a) authority
  b) leniency
  c) sincerity
  d) harshness

19. fresco
  a) painting done on canvas
  b) religious painting
  c) French painting
  d) painting done on plaster

20. oratory
  a) small room for prayer
  b) kitchen in a convent
  c) lobby or vestibule
  d) work room in a convent

Writing Down My Childhood Memories	# Chapter 11	Text Pages 108-120

Perfect Score: 100   Score: _____

1. indebted to
  a) owing thanks to
  b) directed by
  c) nourished by
  d) mindful of

2. progress
  a) move
  b) increase
  c) advance
  d) change

3. abandonment
  a) self-improvement
  b) self-surrender
  c) humiliation
  d) perfection

4. chanced upon
  a) planned to establish
  b) taught
  c) happened to discover
  d) prepared to teach

5. mount
  a) walk on
  b) climb down
  c) find
  d) climb up

6. sanctity
  a) holiness
  b) faith
  c) fortitude
  d) purity

7. **solely**
   a) trustingly
   b) only
   c) faithfully
   d) particularly

8. **trifles**
   a) holy desires
   b) daily duties
   c) harmless things
   d) very little things

9. **possess**
   a) abide by
   b) practice
   c) own
   d) live

10. **undertaking**
    a) aspect, part
    b) task, enterprise
    c) situation, circumstance
    d) aim, goal

11. **glazed** (eyes)
    a) glassy
    b) clear
    c) sharp
    d) watery

12. **bliss**
    a) supreme happiness
    b) eternity
    c) supreme beauty
    d) salvation

13. **rigorous**
    a) spiritual
    b) strict
    c) plain
    d) bold

14. **objection**
    a) rejection
    b) question
    c) protest
    d) explanation

15. **grounds**
    a) basis
    b) preparation
    c) guarantee
    d) protest

16. **resigned to**
    a) in agreement with
    b) accepting of
    c) informed about
    d) enthusiastic about

17. **withdraws**
    a) puts forward
    b) relies upon
    c) maintains
    d) takes back

18. **profoundly**
    a) spiritually
    b) deeply
    c) comfortingly
    d) affectionately

19. **intercession**
    a) obtaining a favor on behalf of another
    b) obtaining a favor for oneself
    c) acts of penance and mortification
    d) eternal happiness

20. **summoned**
    a) brought
    b) led
    c) called
    d) escorted

My Little
Way

Chapter 12

Text
Pages
121-129

Perfect Score: 100   Score: _____

1. related
   a) announced
   b) told
   c) declared
   d) remembered

2. submitted
   a) rehearsed
   b) turned in
   c) enrolled
   d) mailed

3. of attainment
   a) to reach, obtain
   b) to complete, perfect
   c) to understand, learn
   d) to sanctify, make holy

4. infinite
   a) intense
   b) constant
   c) unlimited
   d) enormous

5. mankind
   a) all male human beings
   b) all adult human beings
   c) all human beings
   d) all Christians

6. immense
   a) constant, never-ending
   b) intense, strong
   c) trustworthy, loyal
   d) enormous, immeasurable

7. atone for
   a) make amends for
   b) convert
   c) assist spiritually
   d) save

8. penetration
   a) action of burning intensely
   b) action of entering deeply
   c) action of gripping firmly
   d) action of overwhelming

9. pertaining to
   a) leading up to
   b) helpful to
   c) relating to
   d) similar to

10. merit
   a) discover by God's grace
   b) earn by God's grace
   c) believe by God's grace
   d) love by God's grace

11. channel
   a) source or foundation of something
   b) destination of something
   c) route through which something
         passes
   d) cause of something

12. retired
   a) retracted
   b) withheld
   c) withdrew
   d) returned

13. literary
   a) relating to intellectual discussions
   b) relating to theology
   c) relating to spirituality
   d) relating to books and writings

14. masterpiece
   a) great work
   b) famous work
   c) popular work
   d) good work

15. **successor**
    a) a person who holds a position before another does
    b) a person who holds a position after another does
    c) a person who has been elected to serve in a position
    d) a person who shares a position with another

16. **welfare**
    a) approval
    b) instruction
    c) good
    d) favor

17. **namely**
    a) that is
    b) more importantly
    c) for example
    d) including

18. **acquire**
    a) experience
    b) accomplish
    c) learn
    d) gain

19. **humiliation**
    a) something that hurts one's humility
    b) something that hurts one's pride
    c) something that causes disease
    d) something that causes one to grow in generosity

20. **token**
    a) act of apology
    b) gift that represents something
    c) act of reverence and respect
    d) just payment

A Wonderful Dream and
A Terrible Temptation

Chapter 13

Perfect Score: 100   Score: _____

1. **repository**
    a) side altar where the Blessed Sacrament is placed on Holy Thursday
    b) side altar where the Blessed Sacrament is placed on Good Friday
    c) side altar where the Blessed Sacrament is placed on Holy Saturday
    d) side altar where the Blessed Sacrament is placed on Easter Sunday

2. **mortify**
    a) subdue
    b) ignore
    c) endure
    d) satisfy

3. **harvest**
    a) planting of seed
    b) cultivating of young crops
    c) gathering of ripened crops
    d) marketing of new produce

4. **observances**
    a) responsibilities, obligations
    b) observations
    c) vows, promises
    d) customary practices, ceremonies

5. **zest**
    a) enthusiasm and enjoyment
    b) obedience, submission
    c) strictness, exactness
    d) devotion and piety

6. **fatigue**
   a) pain, suffering
   b) sorrow, grief
   c) sickness, illness
   d) tiredness, exhaustion

7. **withdrew**
   a) returned
   b) worried
   c) retired
   d) withheld

8. **fell prey to**
   a) became a victim of
   b) developed
   c) was found to have
   d) showed signs of

9. **Indochina**
   a) central area of China
   b) island northeast of China
   c) nation between India and China
   d) peninsula of Southeast Asia

10. **reform**
    a) missionary movement
    b) change of an organization's location
    c) change of an organization's leadership
    d) amendment, correction

11. **convey**
    a) convince
    b) make certain
    c) communicate
    d) imagine

12. **consolation**
    a) obligation, duty
    b) practice of virtue
    c) mission, calling
    d) spiritual comfort and joy

13. **brethren** (literal meaning)
    a) sinners
    b) persons
    c) friends
    d) brothers

14. **in accordance with**
    a) in expectation of
    b) in honor of
    c) in agreement with
    d) in the midst of

15. **confided**
    a) kept secret
    b) entrusted
    c) carefully discussed
    d) publicly announced

16. **gay**
    a) cheerful, lighthearted
    b) kind, gracious
    c) comical, humorous
    d) talkative, chatty

17. **borne**
    a) realized
    b) performed
    c) endured
    d) obtained

18. **Blessed** (title before a person's name)
    a) one who has been beatified
    b) one who has been canonized
    c) one who has been consecrated a Bishop
    d) The Holy Father

19. **the Orient**
    a) the Far East
    b) Europe
    c) the Middle East
    d) Africa

20. **gravely**
    a) with resignation
    b) very seriously
    c) very anxiously
    d) with humility

Mysterious
Promises

Chapter 14

Text
Pages
142-152

Perfect Score: 100   **Score:** _____

1. **anxiety**
   a) expense, cost
   b) sadness, sorrow
   c) worry, distress
   d) time

2. **infirmary**
   a) place of lodging and care for the
       sick
   b) emergency room
   c) clinic
   d) any place of care

3. **submit**
   a) comply
   b) suffer
   c) offer up
   d) act

4. **prescribed**
   a) allowed, permitted
   b) ordered, dictated
   c) evaluated, checked
   d) utilized, used

5. **circular** (letter, notice, etc.)
   a) intended to be confidential
   b) periodical
   c) intended to be passed around
   d) official

6. **amiable**
   a) sincere, earnest
   b) smart, intelligent
   c) helpful, useful
   d) pleasant, friendly

7. **lot**
   a) destiny
   b) hope
   c) life
   d) choice

8. **ambitious**
   a) stealthily seeking wealth by
       dishonest means
   b) pridefully considering oneself better
       than others
   c) lazily allowing others to do all the
       work
   d) ardently desiring to advance
       one's own interests

9. **iniquity**
   a) wickedness
   b) covetousness
   c) selfishness
   d) mischievousness

10. **refrain from**
    a) begin to
    b) continue
    c) keep from
    d) give up

11. **vigorously**
    a) carefully
    b) energetically
    c) carelessly
    d) continuously

12. **pretexts**
    a) ways
    b) good reasons
    c) thoughts
    d) excuses

13. **yielding to**
    a) agreeing with
    b) giving in to
    c) clinging to
    d) embracing

14. capacity
 a) quest
 b) desire
 c) potential
 d) understanding

15. noble
 a) special
 b) pious
 c) innocent
 d) honorable

16. existence
 a) talents, abilities
 b) graces, blessings
 c) being, life
 d) virtues, merits

17. renounced
 a) abandoned
 b) accepted
 c) rejected
 d) realized

18. repose
 a) happiness
 b) rest
 c) activity
 d) restoration

19. the elect
 a) priests, nuns and religious brothers
 b) those who are going to Heaven
 c) those who are spiritually advanced
 d) those who are canonized or beatified

20. discern
 a) detect, recognize
 b) appreciate, be grateful for
 c) explain, expound on
 d) be loyal to

God Calls
Me to Heaven

Chapter 15

Perfect Score: 100　　　　　　　　　　　　**Score:** _____

1. scarcely
 a) definitely
 b) necessarily
 c) hardly
 d) almost

2. ever-present
 a) sometimes present
 b) always present
 c) never present
 d) nearly present

3. manifest
 a) merited
 b) shown
 c) sanctified
 d) chosen

4. undergo
 a) understand
 b) discover
 c) endure
 d) choose

5. upheld
 a) taught
 b) led
 c) surrounded
 d) supported

6. published
 a) recorded in a library or archive
 b) made into a book and distributed
 c) hand-copied by a calligrapher
 d) decorated with artwork

7. **snares**
   a) detours
   b) traps
   c) dangers
   d) obstacles

8. **inserted**
   a) put in
   b) took out
   c) emphasized
   d) expanded

9. **multitude**
   a) infinity
   b) mass
   c) great number
   d) immorality

10. **cast**
    a) thrown
    b) added
    c) dropped
    d) placed

11. **wrought**
    a) begun
    b) worked
    c) prevented
    d) harmed

12. **Eternal Life**
    a) devotion
    b) perfection
    c) heaven
    d) virtue

13. **hastened**
    a) wanted
    b) attempted
    c) decided
    d) hurried

14. **turret**
    a) a small tower
    b) a small window
    c) a small room
    d) a small balcony

15. **fortified**
    a) made strong
    b) well hidden
    c) well situated
    d) difficult to escape from

16. **vigilance**
    a) keen vision
    b) watchfulness
    c) memory
    d) judgment

17. **confiding**
    a) conversing
    b) trusting
    c) confining
    d) loving

18. **despair**
    a) the giving up of faith
    b) the giving up of hope
    c) state of discouragement
    d) state of bewilderment

19. **sow** (literal meaning)
    a) plant
    b) cultivate
    c) harvest
    d) market

20. **onslaughts**
    a) tricks
    b) lies
    c) attacks
    d) obstructions

Instructions: Circle the letter of the answer which best matches the meaning of the vocabulary word.

A Child Is Born	# Chapter 1	Text Pages 1-11

Perfect Score: 100   Score: _____

1. deftly
   a) swiftly
   b) skillfully
   c) in a complicated pattern
   d) coarsely

2. merchant
   a) one who raises animals
   b) one who buys and sells goods
   c) one who manages a restaurant
   d) one who makes clothing

3. rash
   a) reckless
   b) selfish
   c) clever
   d) thoughtful

4. lamely
   a) convincingly
   b) powerfully
   c) weakly
   d) humorously

5. failing
   a) petition
   b) desire
   c) fault
   d) habit

6. destination
   a) place where people pray
   b) place where one lives
   c) place from which someone has come
   d) place to which someone is going

7. courteous
   a) careless
   b) thoughtless
   c) obedient
   d) polite

8. quarters
   a) where one lives
   b) homeless shelters
   c) where one works
   d) uncomfortable rooms

9. resolutely
   a) decisively
   b) thoughtfully
   c) immediately
   d) waveringly

10. Donna (title before a name)
   a) Madam
   b) Your Highness
   c) Miss
   d) Princess

11. prominent
  a) unimportant
  b) hidden, concealed
  c) noticeable, standing out
  d) first in line

12. motley
  a) mixed, miscellaneous-looking
  b) loud or rowdy
  c) consisting of tramps and beggars
  d) consisting of many people

13. clamor
  a) melodic chiming
  b) beautiful tune
  c) loud, continuous noise
  d) announcement, declaration

14. recess
  a) hollow, indented space
  b) space shaped like a circle
  c) large room
  d) hiding place

15. frail
  a) elderly
  b) poorly clothed
  c) physically weak
  d) absent-minded

16. ambassador
  a) president
  b) representative
  c) merchant
  d) banker

17. render
  a) cleanse
  b) sanctify
  c) bless
  d) make

18. fervently
  a) ardently, wholeheartedly
  b) simply, straightforwardly
  c) happily, joyfully
  d) quickly, briskly

19. festive
  a) charming, fascinating
  b) made of rich fabric
  c) holiday-like
  d) multi-colored

20. bid
  a) act as host toward guests
  b) invite or command to do something
  c) give or share one's goods
  d) forbid or prohibit from doing something

<table>
<tr><td>The Dream</td><td>Chapter 2</td><td>Text Pages 12-22</td></tr>
</table>

Perfect Score: 100   Score: _____

1. unaccustomed
  a) not usual
  b) not planned
  c) complimentary, free
  d) generous, abundant

2. flares
  a) candles
  b) torches
  c) lamps
  d) light bulbs

3. revelry
  a) arguing
  b) activity
  c) merrymaking
  d) happiness

4. slumber
  a) dreaming
  b) travel
  c) rest
  d) sleep

5. nobility
   a) artists and poets
   b) persons of high rank in society
   c) persons of the middle class
   d) warriors, soldiers

6. peculiar
   a) strange
   b) stylish
   c) interesting
   d) outdated

7. century
   a) period of ten years
   b) period of 100 years
   c) period of 500 years
   d) period of 1000 years

8. clad
   a) poorly clothed
   b) clothed
   c) disguised
   d) wearing a religious habit

9. scanned
   a) looked at with affection
   b) examined thoroughly
   c) ignored
   d) looked over quickly

10. commotion
   a) noisy disturbance
   b) horse and wagon accident
   c) argument
   d) procession of people

11. whereupon
   a) after which
   b) before which
   c) in which
   d) under which

12. founder
   a) one who first establishes
   b) one who leads
   c) the most famous member
   d) the most popular member

13. transported
   a) built, constructed
   b) found, discovered
   c) moved, carried
   d) driven, pushed

14. murmured
   a) said softly
   b) said slowly
   c) said quickly
   d) said clearly

15. anxiously
   a) hurriedly
   b) worriedly
   c) impatiently
   d) angrily

16. vigorously
   a) quickly
   b) unexpectedly
   c) immediately
   d) forcefully

17. reproachful
   a) resentful, angry
   b) insulting, rude
   c) disapproving, blaming
   d) upset, frustrated

18. theology
   a) the study of things relating to God
   b) the study of human behavior
   c) the study of things relating to
      dreams
   d) the study of things relating to
      motherhood

19. heresy
   a) drunkenness
   b) false religious belief
   c) wicked life
   d) disgrace

20. aim
   a) desire
   b) accomplishment
   c) goal
   d) fame

Another
Birthday

Chapter 3

Text
Pages
23-34

Perfect Score: 100   Score: _____

1. lilting
   a) random and choppy
   b) cheerful and rhythmic
   c) slow and flowing
   d) loud and disturbing

2. dwelling
   a) place where one works
   b) place where one lives
   c) place where one waits
   d) place where one visits

3. temples
   a) creatures
   b) children
   c) obedient servants
   d) holy dwelling places

4. devoutly
   a) quietly
   b) thoughtfully
   c) piously
   d) slowly

5. dismay
   a) boredom
   b) alarm
   c) outrage
   d) surprise

6. elaborate
   a) expensive
   b) short and simple
   c) fancy and complicated
   d) delicious

7. tapestries
   a) fabrics interwoven with pictures
   b) paintings done on canvas
   c) paintings done on the wall; murals
   d) any works of art

8. hearth
   a) the floor of a fireplace
   b) a hot grill
   c) a cast-iron stove
   d) a heating device

9. affection
   a) admiration, praise
   b) jealousy
   c) love, tenderness
   d) pride

10. crucifix
   a) cross
   b) cross on a rosary
   c) cross with an image of Christ
        crucified
   d) gold cross

11. caressed
   a) admired
   b) held tightly
   c) stroked with affection
   d) looked at closely

12. the Orient
   a) the northern part of the world
   b) the southern part of the world
   c) the eastern part of the world
   d) the western part of the world

13. wistful
   a) in a light-hearted, joyful manner
   b) in a decisive, vigorous manner
   c) in a sad, grief-stricken manner
   d) in a thoughtful, wishful manner

14. solemn
   a) serious, grave
   b) kind, sweet
   c) sorrowful, sad
   d) hopeful

15. astonished
a) embarrassed
b) amazed
c) reluctant
d) puzzled

16. awkwardly
a) excitedly, eagerly
b) backwards
c) uneasily, clumsily
d) with annoyance

17. twined
a) twisted
b) tied
c) rolled
d) pulled

18. abruptly
a) angrily, furiously
b) curtly, brusquely
c) gently, kindly
d) jokingly, teasingly

19. quivering
a) chattering
b) quiet
c) high-pitched
d) trembling

20. boastfully
a) in a dishonest manner
b) in a belligerent manner
c) in a greedy manner
d) in a bragging manner

The Dominicans
in Bologna

Chapter 4

Text
Pages
35-47

Perfect Score: 100

Score: _____

1. persecution
a) unjust treatment
b) investigation
c) purification
d) battle

2. martyr
a) person who is killed
b) person who dies for Christ
c) person who lives for Christ
d) saintly young person

3. catacombs
a) buildings where Christians
worshiped in secret
b) towers where Christians worshiped
in secret
c) networks of dirt roads connecting
Christian homes
d) underground places of Christian
burial and worship

4. doctrine
a) prayer
b) holiness
c) power
d) teaching

5. Communion of Saints
a) Sacraments and sacramentals
b) Catholics on earth, in Purgatory,
and in Heaven
c) those who are beatified or canonized
d) priests, nuns, and brothers

6. binding
a) encouraging
b) uniting
c) comforting
d) supporting

7. cloistered
a) enclosed
b) teaching
c) consecrated
d) chosen

8. **the Order of Preachers**
   a) the Carmelite Order
   b) the Franciscan Order
   c) the Benedictine Order
   d) the Dominican Order

9. **was fostered**
   a) was encouraged
   b) was explained
   c) was begun
   d) was tolerated

10. **clever**
    a) dishonest, deceitful
    b) good at telling jokes
    c) highly educated
    d) smart, talented

11. **friars**
    a) brothers or sisters in certain religious orders
    b) brothers in certain religious orders
    c) students at a university
    d) teachers at a university

12. **stormed**
    a) destroyed
    b) set fire to
    c) attacked
    d) tore down

13. **charge**
    a) pupil or student
    b) someone committed to another's care
    c) someone who takes care of others
    d) helper

14. **rheumatism**
    a) a type of cancer
    b) a disorder resulting in the loss of the ability to think clearly
    c) a disorder of the joints or muscles
    d) a disease resulting in loss of sight

15. **save**
    a) except
    b) around
    c) before
    d) after

16. **ceased**
    a) stopped
    b) started
    c) grew louder
    d) grew softer

17. **Vespers**
    a) midnight prayer of the Divine Office
    b) evening prayer of the Divine Office
    c) midday prayer of the Divine Office
    d) morning prayer of the Divine Office

18. **decked**
    a) decorated
    b) decorated with boughs of holly
    c) arranged
    d) scented

19. **inscription**
    a) words painted on a wall
    b) religious words
    c) words carved on a hard surface
    d) famous words

20. **migrated**
    a) received a reward
    b) moved somewhere else
    c) bowed in reverence
    d) practiced great obedience

A New
Life

Chapter 5

Text
Pages
48-59

Perfect Score: 100   Score: _____

1. **cloister**
   a) convent of teaching sisters
   b) enclosed convent or monastery
   c) old convent or monastery
   d) famous convent or monastery

2. **ardent**
   a) constant
   b) willing
   c) pure
   d) fervent

3. **gravely**
   a) slowly
   b) sorrowfully
   c) seriously
   d) carefully

4. **hardships**
   a) hunger and thirst
   b) penance, mortifications
   c) long prayers at night
   d) difficulties, sufferings

5. **scarce**
   a) of poor quality
   b) in short supply
   c) non-existent
   d) sufficient

6. **yielded**
   a) gave in
   b) dominated
   c) understood
   d) conquered one's feelings

7. **threshold**
   a) front porch
   b) cloister
   c) sill of a doorway
   d) lawn, yard

8. **falter**
   a) hesitate
   b) sniffle
   c) reverse one's course
   d) sob

9. **assembled**
   a) gathered together
   b) lined up
   c) spread out
   d) put on display

10. **inquired**
    a) asked
    b) began
    c) demanded
    d) stated

11. **tunic**
    a) long, pleated garment
    b) straight, gown-like garment
    c) fancy embroidered garment
    d) cloak

12. **scapular**
    a) cord or rope worn around the waist
    b) broad band of cloth worn in front
       and back over the shoulders
    c) full-length cloak with a hood
       attached to it
    d) sandals, open footwear

13. **novice**
    a) new Sister preparing to receive the
       religious habit
    b) new Sister who has already received
       the religious habit
    c) Sister who comes from a noble
       family
    d) Sister who is under age 17

14. **persevere**
   a) persist despite obstacles
   b) make a good impression
   c) make a good preparation
   d) make a good beginning

15. **refectory**
   a) waiting room in a convent, monastery or seminary
   b) recreation room in a convent, monastery or seminary
   c) dining room in a convent, monastery or seminary
   d) parlor in a convent, monastery or seminary

16. **humiliations**
   a) circumstances that make one proud
   b) circumstances that cause one's pride to suffer
   c) spiritual exercises for novices
   d) prayers recited in the refectory

17. **crude**
   a) hateful
   b) rough
   c) frightening
   d) ugly

18. **shrewdly**
   a) sadly, sorrowfully
   b) in a low tone of voice
   c) teasingly, jokingly
   d) cleverly, wisely

19. **timid**
   a) lacking in respect
   b) overwhelmed
   c) lacking in confidence
   d) surprised

20. **glistening**
   a) bright
   b) shining
   c) clanking, clattering
   d) golden

The Miracle | **Chapter 6** | Text Pages 60-71

Perfect Score: 100   Score: _____

1. **sentiments**
   a) facts
   b) feelings
   c) theories
   d) questions

2. **intercede**
   a) praise, glorify
   b) take an interest in someone else's need
   c) make a request on behalf of another
   d) make a request for oneself

3. **literary**
   a) pertaining to art
   b) pertaining to historical research
   c) pertaining to prose and poetry
   d) pertaining to music

4. **Rhineland**
   a) area of France west of the Rhine River
   b) area of France west of the Rhine Mountains
   c) area of Germany west of the Rhine River
   d) area of Germany west of the Rhine Mountains

5. **has enlightened**
   a) has commanded
   b) has called
   c) has given holiness to
   d) has given understanding to

VOCABULARY QUIZ WORKBOOK

6. **consoled**
   a) comforted
   b) inspired
   c) rejected
   d) discouraged

7. **vigil**
   a) the day before a feast day
   b) the day after a feast day
   c) the period of eight days after a feast day
   d) the evening of a feast day

8. **obscured**
   a) secured
   b) reported
   c) hidden
   d) separated

9. **reverently**
   a) in a quiet and thoughtful manner
   b) in a deeply respectful manner
   c) in a considerate manner
   d) with meditation

10. **customary**
    a) opening
    b) closing
    c) devout
    d) usual

11. **prostrated**
    a) knelt reverently
    b) lay facedown
    c) sat motionless
    d) bowed from the waist

12. **Confiteor**
    a) prayer that begins "I believe . . ."
    b) prayer that begins "I confess . . ."
    c) prayer that begins "I adore . . ."
    d) prayer that begins "I love . . ."

13. **carefree**
    a) without responsibilities or worry
    b) without common sense
    c) innocent, sinless
    d) pleasant, enjoyable

14. **mourn**
    a) complain
    b) daydream
    c) meditate
    d) grieve

15. **suspended**
    a) pulled forward
    b) illuminated
    c) held up
    d) moved

16. **consecrated** (Host)
    a) representing the Body and Blood of Christ
    b) changed into the Body and Blood of Christ
    c) reminding one of the Body and Blood of Christ
    d) similar to the Body and Blood of Christ

17. **unhindered**
    a) slowly and carefully
    b) without interference
    c) with a circular motion
    d) in an unearthly manner

18. **rapture**
    a) sudden overwhelming joy
    b) great supernatural virtue
    c) utter bewilderment
    d) fear and trembling

19. **prolonged**
    a) unexpected
    b) unexplained
    c) extended
    d) authoritative

20. **ecstasy**
    a) overwhelming experience of joy
    b) perfectly upright posture
    c) perfect obedience
    d) very fervent prayer of petition

Little
Saint

Chapter 7

Text
Pages
72-82

Perfect Score: 100   Score: _____

1. departure
   a) the act of praying
   b) the act of saying good-bye
   c) the act of leaving
   d) the act of kneeling

2. immense
   a) constant, never-ending
   b) vast, huge
   c) intense
   d) holy

3. novice mistress
   a) sister who cares for the chapel
   b) sister who guides the new sisters
   c) Mother Superior of the convent
   d) Mother General of the Order

4. hasten (the day)
   a) bless
   b) command to come
   c) cause to come
   d) cause to come soon

5. absorbed
   a) occupied
   b) engrossed
   c) distracted
   d) busy

6. weariness
   a) silence
   b) stiffness
   c) stillness
   d) tiredness

7. thoroughly
   a) suddenly
   b) obviously
   c) completely
   d) with bewilderment

8. breathtaking
   a) astonishing, thrilling
   b) joyful, happy
   c) unlikely, doubtful
   d) scandalous, demoralizing

9. flocked
   a) made a short journey
   b) traveled despite obstacles
   c) gathered or went in a crowd
   d) went one by one

10. clamored for
   a) spread the story of
   b) questioned
   c) cheered
   d) demanded loudly

11. prioress
   a) nun in charge of a monastery
   b) nun in charge of novices
   c) nun who serves as doorkeeper
   d) nun who cares for the sacristy

12. conviction
   a) the state of being determined
   b) the state of feeling stubborn
   c) the state of being persuasive
   d) the state of feeling certain

13. uttered
   a) whispered
   b) said softly
   c) spoke
   d) thought to oneself

14. grieved
   a) dismayed
   b) disappointed
   c) sorrowful
   d) slightly upset

15. **restraining**
    a) encouraging
    b) holding back
    c) commanding
    d) inviting

16. **onlookers**
    a) spies
    b) observers
    c) well-wishers
    d) guests

17. **withdrew**
    a) moved away
    b) sat down
    c) bowed
    d) stopped

18. **marveled**
    a) realized, understood
    b) remembered, recalled
    c) thought with sorrow
    d) thought with amazement

19. **sanctuary**
    a) the part of a church where the people sit
    b) the part of a church where the priests vest
    c) the part of a church where the high altar stands
    d) the part of a church where the Sacrament of Penance is received

20. **deter**
    a) encourage, urge onward
    b) fill with confidence
    c) help, assist
    d) hold back, prevent

BOOK FIVE
THE MIRACULOUS MEDAL

Instructions: Circle the letter of the answer which best matches the meaning of the vocabulary word.

Our Lady Comes to
Sister Catherine

Chapter 1

Text
Pages
1-5

Perfect Score: 100

Score: _____

1. **gleamed**
   a) brightened
   b) dazed
   c) dazzled
   d) shone

2. **cafes**
   a) small grocery stores
   b) small hotels
   c) small restaurants
   d) small specialty shops

3. **motherhouse**
   a) house for widowed mothers
   b) main convent
   c) convent where the poor are served
   d) convent where children are taught

4. **presently**
   a) later
   b) afterwards
   c) soon
   d) slowly

5. **stirred**
   a) rolled over
   b) moved slightly
   c) jumped up
   d) sat up

6. **start**
   a) jerk
   b) bump
   c) sigh
   d) movement

7. **dormitory**
   a) room where a number of people work
   b) room where a number of people pray
   c) room where a number of people meet
   d) room where a number of people sleep

8. **scarcely**
   a) almost
   b) hardly
   c) definitely
   d) necessarily

9. **corridors**
   a) rooms
   b) hallways
   c) stairways
   d) large spaces

10. **reveal**
    a) show
    b) hide
    c) turn on
    d) create

11. ablaze
a) burning brightly
b) flickering on and off
c) glowing faintly
d) casting shadows

12. chaplain
a) priest who helps run the diocese
b) priest who is pastor of a parish
c) priest who goes door to door begging for the poor
d) priest who takes care of souls at a convent or school

13. accustomed to
a) in the habit of
b) expected to
c) known to
d) ordered to

14. addressing
a) viewing
b) listening to
c) speaking to
d) taking attendance

15. attracted
a) confused
b) displeased
c) annoyed
d) drawn

16. rustling
a) rubbing
b) swishing
c) pounding
d) touching

17. reassuringly
a) in a grave, serious manner
b) in a very respectful manner
c) in a manner of restoring confidence
d) in a manner of casting doubt

18. misgivings
a) hesitations
b) ideas
c) faith
d) sleepiness

19. sanctuary
a) part of a church where the high altar stands
b) part of a church where the priest vests
c) part of a church where Baptism is administered
d) part of a church where sacred vessels are kept

20. gracious
a) majestic
b) queenly
c) beautiful
d) kind

Father Aladel Does
Not Believe

The Vision of
the Medal

Chapters 2, 3

Text
Pages
6-15

Perfect Score: 100   Score: _____

1. **trial**
   a) difficulty, trouble
   b) illness, sickness
   c) war, fighting
   d) sin, unfaithfulness

2. **charge**
   a) inspire
   b) test
   c) entrust
   d) encourage

3. **bear**
   a) enjoy
   b) seek
   c) understand
   d) endure

4. **contradicted**
   a) disturbed
   b) opposed
   c) injured
   d) hurt

5. **persecuted**
   a) scandalized
   b) publicized
   c) harassed
   d) cursed

6. **laity**
   a) unmarried Catholics
   b) people who are not Christian
   c) Catholics who are not ordained
   d) married Catholics

7. **indicated**
   a) proclaimed
   b) ordered
   c) whispered
   d) signalled

8. **interview**
   a) meditation
   b) meeting
   c) experience
   d) vision

9. **dismay**
   a) disappointment, anxiety
   b) disgrace, dishonor
   c) anger, fury
   d) annoyance, irritation

10. **informed**
    a) gave advice to
    b) gave knowledge to
    c) gave praise to
    d) gave a warning to

11. **protested**
    a) said, remarked
    b) interrupted, interfered
    c) objected, argued
    d) grumbled, complained

----

12. **concerned**
    a) discussed
    b) involved
    c) responsible
    d) told

13. **scandal**
    a) excitement
    b) sadness
    c) publicity
    d) disgrace

14. resembled
a) reflected
b) was similar to
c) was better than
d) was the same as

15. surmounted with
a) blessed by
b) attached to
c) adorned with
d) topped with

16. ecstasy
a) profound obedience
b) deep respect
c) complete silence
d) overwhelming joy

17. heedless of
a) courteous to
b) discourteous to
c) mindful of
d) unmindful of

18. enveloped
a) protected
b) surrounded
c) brightened
d) adorned

19. abound
a) be available in small quantity
b) be available in average-size quantity
c) be available in great quantity
d) be available at regular intervals

20. encircled by
a) beside a circle of
b) connected to a circle of
c) on top of a circle of
d) surrounded by a circle of

Father Aladel
Still Hesitates

Father Aladel
Finally Consents

Chapters 4, 5

Perfect Score: 100

Score: _____

1. emphatically
a) rudely, hurtfully
b) forcefully, insistently
c) doubtfully, uncertainly
d) frankly, candidly

2. undertake
a) attempt
b) complete
c) undergo
d) order

3. novice
a) religious brother or sister preparing to take vows
b) religious brother or sister who does kitchen work
c) religious brother or sister under the age of 18
d) religious brother or sister who comes from a poor family

VOCABULARY QUIZ WORKBOOK

4. **vision**
   a) something heard in a mysterious, spiritual way
   b) something seen in a mysterious, spiritual way
   c) something felt in a mysterious, spiritual way
   d) something thought in a mysterious, spiritual way

5. **fancies**
   a) lies, deceitful statements
   b) pride and stubbornness
   c) acts of disobedience
   d) imaginings, foolish ideas

6. **in earnest**
   a) serious
   b) pious
   c) gracious
   d) virtuous

7. **consoled**
   a) encouraged
   b) distracted
   c) emboldened
   d) comforted

8. **novitiate**
   a) time spent making a novena
   b) time spent as a postulant
   c) time spent as a novice
   d) time spent preparing to become a novice

9. **conceived without sin**
   a) free from original sin from the first moment of one's existence
   b) free from original sin from the moment of one's birth
   c) having had original sin removed from one's soul by Baptism
   d) not guilty of any actual sin

10. **have recourse to**
    a) go to for help
    b) remember or commemorate
    c) imitate the virtues of
    d) praise and venerate

11. **affairs**
    a) misunderstandings
    b) arguments, fights
    c) events, concerns
    d) problems, trials

12. **refrained from**
    a) been inclined toward
    b) kept from
    c) disapproved of
    d) been inclined against

---

13. **merit**
    a) grace
    b) blessing
    c) sincerity
    d) worth

14. **sought out**
    a) looked for
    b) questioned
    c) called for
    d) consulted

15. **suburb**
    a) region in the center of a city
    b) region just outside a city
    c) region on the north side of a city
    d) region in the business district of a city

16. **departure**
    a) the act of arriving
    b) the act of leaving
    c) the act of moving
    d) the act of receiving an assignment

17. stoop to (figurative meaning)
    a) make a practice of
    b) lower oneself by
    c) make an attempt at
    d) commit the offense of

18. sensible
    a) reasonable
    b) obedient
    c) virtuous
    d) self-disciplined

19. inclined to
    a) failing to
    b) feeling pressured to
    c) tending to
    d) hesitant to

20. abruptly
    a) surprisingly
    b) suddenly
    c) with strong feeling
    d) angrily

The Bishop
Says Yes

Finding the
Right Picture

Chapters 6, 7

Text
Pages
26-33

Perfect Score: 100

Score: _____

1. objection
    a) apology
    b) protest
    c) assistance
    d) advice

2. inquired
    a) asked
    b) commented
    c) declared
    d) demanded

3. with bated breath
    a) patiently
    b) nervously
    c) with annoyance
    d) in suspense

4. latter
    a) the first person or thing of two
       mentioned
    b) the second person or thing of two
       mentioned
    c) the higher-ranking person or thing
       of two mentioned
    d) the lower-ranking person or thing
       of two mentioned

5. forthcoming
    a) short and to the point
    b) exciting
    c) appearing soon
    d) satisfying, worthwhile

6. (eyes) clouded (figurative meaning)
    a) closed
    b) squinted
    c) expressed interest
    d) expressed distress

7. account
    a) view
    b) opinion
    c) attitude
    d) report

8. confide in
    a) give advice to
    b) give secret information to
    c) obey
    d) listen to

     VOCABULARY QUIZ WORKBOOK

9. **save**
   a) around
   b) except
   c) involving
   d) related to

10. **in confidence**
    a) devoutly
    b) as a secret
    c) as a summary report
    d) respectfully

11. **revolution**
    a) rule by a tyrant
    b) election of a tyrant
    c) persecution of the Church
    d) overthrow of the government

12. **dethroned**
    a) removed from power
    b) voted out of office
    c) killed or imprisoned
    d) replaced

13. **godless**
    a) tyrannical
    b) not acknowledging God
    c) hungry for power
    d) sacrilegious

----

14. **in due course**
    a) eventually
    b) thankfully
    c) lawfully
    d) soon

15. **apparent**
    a) disturbing
    b) burdensome
    c) discouraging
    d) obvious

16. **radiance**
    a) beauty
    b) uniqueness
    c) brilliance
    d) attractiveness

17. **insoluble**
    a) unable to be understood
    b) challenging
    c) unable to be solved
    d) frustrating

18. **gasp**
    a) a sudden gesture
    b) a sudden, short breath
    c) a sigh
    d) a sudden cry

19. **acknowledged**
    a) mentioned
    b) admitted
    c) announced
    d) promised

20. **reverently**
    a) admiringly
    b) uncertainly
    c) enthusiastically
    d) respectfully

The Medal Becomes
Known as "The
Miraculous Medal"

Obstinate Old John

Chapters 8, 9

Text
Pages
34-44

Perfect Score: 100   Score: _____

1. **conviction**
    a) uncertainty
    b) strong desire
    c) firm belief
    d) announcement

2. **exhausted**
    a) used up
    b) in need
    c) necessary
    d) inadequate

3. **cholera**
    a) serious disease of the stomach
       and intestines
    b) serious disease of the heart and
       blood vessels
    c) serious disease of the muscles and
       joints
    d) serious disease of the brain and
       nerves

4. **contributed**
    a) discussed
    b) suggested
    c) conjectured
    d) added

5. **idle** (talk)
    a) forbidden
    b) secretive
    c) useless
    d) unkind

6. **apparitions**
    a) experiences
    b) miracles
    c) visions
    d) prophecies

7. **advertising**
    a) calling attention to
    b) forcing onto others
    c) keeping secret
    d) making use of

8. **piety**
    a) liberty, freedom
    b) religious devotion
    c) personal adornment
    d) shyness, bashfulness

9. **banish**
    a) punish
    b) imprison
    c) terrorize
    d) expel

10. **outright**
    a) hateful
    b) unlawful
    c) harmful, dangerous
    d) open, actual

11. **well-nigh**
    a) almost
    b) definitely
    c) probably
    d) doubtlessly

12. obstinate
   a) mean
   b) ill-tempered, rude
   c) stubborn
   d) irreligious

13. infirmary
   a) interior of the building
   b) place where the sick are treated
      and dismissed
   c) place of lodging and care for the sick
   d) dormitory, room for sleeping

14. disagreeable
   a) stubborn
   b) in pain
   c) disappointing
   d) unpleasant

15. barring
   a) except for
   b) after
   c) with
   d) asking for

16. whim
   a) evil idea
   b) senseless wish
   c) stubborn mood
   d) obnoxious behavior

17. resume
   a) exaggerate
   b) end
   c) continue
   d) tell

18. relating
   a) proclaiming
   b) telling
   c) declaring
   d) announcing

19. vocation
   a) life
   b) education
   c) plan of action
   d) divine call

20. beckoned
   a) intended to dismiss
   b) intended to summon
   c) made a gesture of dismissal
   d) made a gesture of summoning

Sister Catherine Continues
Her Story

Old John Finally Agrees
to Wear the Medal

The Graces People
Forget to Ask For

Chapters 10, 11, 12

Text
Pages
45-58

Perfect Score: 100   Score: _____

1. remarkably
   a) definitely
   b) extraordinarily
   c) decidedly
   d) tolerably

2. wretched
   a) fairly poor
   b) bashful, shy
   c) miserably poor
   d) inexperienced

3. circumstances
a) education
b) problem
c) situation
d) job

---

4. prevailed upon
a) gently coaxed
b) succeeded in persuading
c) argued with
d) attempted to persuade

5. discontent
a) discord
b) confusion
c) greed
d) dissatisfaction

6. chiefly
a) mainly
b) almost
c) definitely
d) probably

7. threshold (literal meaning)
a) garden
b) window
c) driveway
d) doorway

8. likeness
a) painting
b) substitute
c) image
d) drawing

9. wryly
a) in a contorted manner
b) in a hopeful manner
c) happily, contentedly
d) shyly, bashfully

---

10. consented
a) agreed
b) desired
c) started
d) remembered

11. converted
a) helped
b) taught
c) accepted
d) changed

12. hardships
a) duties
b) complications
c) difficulties
d) pains

13. meditations
a) visions
b) mental prayers
c) daydreams
d) religious studies

14. martyrdom
a) political problems
b) chaos in the government
c) suffering for one's beliefs
d) death for one's beliefs

15. company
a) presence
b) intelligence
c) usefulness
d) goodness

16. spiritual
a) involving things of the soul
b) involving things of the body
c) involving religious life
d) involving suffering

17. lapse
a) end
b) continue
c) slip
d) begin

18. undoubtedly
   a) unforgettably
   b) certainly
   c) unfortunately
   d) appropriately

19. disposition
   a) reputation, good name
   b) attitude, mental outlook
   c) situation, environment
   d) occasion

20. contented
   a) directed
   b) disgusted
   c) satisfied
   d) overjoyed

Old John Decides to
Go to Confession

The Children
of Mary

Chapters 13, 14

Text
Pages
59-68

Perfect Score: 100   Score: _____

1. glistened
   a) brightened
   b) lit up
   c) extended
   d) sparkled

2. dispatched
   a) sent
   b) sold
   c) given
   d) bought

3. attributed to
   a) blessed by
   b) cured by
   c) patterned on
   d) credited to

4. intercession
   a) atonement for oneself
   b) atonement on behalf of another
   c) petition for oneself
   d) petition on behalf of another

5. accounts
   a) conversations
   b) reports
   c) publicity
   d) miracles

6. devoutly
   a) regularly
   b) piously
   c) frequently
   d) perfectly

7. conceal
   a) hide
   b) handle
   c) stop
   d) prevent

8. astonishment
   a) interest
   b) happiness
   c) amazement
   d) relief

9. self-conscious
   a) disappointed
   b) embarrassed
   c) angry
   d) regretful

10. matter-of-fact
   a) friendly
   b) interested
   c) emotional
   d) unemotional

----

11. promote
   a) oppose
   b) create
   c) encourage
   d) call attention to

12. noting
   a) realizing
   b) noticing
   c) understanding
   d) assuming

13. utterly
   a) nearly
   b) seemingly
   c) absolutely
   d) somewhat

14. wavered
   a) became unsteady
   b) became fanatical
   c) became burdensome
   d) became hidden

15. expectation
   a) probability
   b) excitement
   c) anticipation
   d) imagination

16. found
   a) discover
   b) assist
   c) renew
   d) establish

17. society
   a) school
   b) association
   c) convent
   d) gathering

18. litany
   a) prayer composed of quotations from the Bible
   b) prayer invoking someone by a list of titles
   c) prayer recited either before or after the Rosary
   d) prayer to Our Lady

19. processions
   a) lines of people walking in a ceremonious manner
   b) groups of people walking in a ceremonious manner
   c) groups of people gathered in a ceremonious manner
   d) lines of people standing in a ceremonious manner

20. consecrated to
   a) specially interested in
   b) specially chosen by
   c) specially associated with
   d) specially dedicated to

VOCABULARY QUIZ WORKBOOK

Our Lady Converts an
Anti-Catholic Jew

Chapter 15

Text
Pages
69-75

Perfect Score: 100   Score: _____

1. **generally**
   a) usually
   b) always
   c) never
   d) occasionally

2. **enrolling**
   a) sanctifying
   b) teaching
   c) volunteering
   d) registering

3. **indulgence**
   a) forgiveness of sins
   b) divine assistance, blessing
   c) remission of spiritual debt
   d) merit for good works performed

4. **affiliated**
   a) controlled
   b) associated
   c) managed
   d) guided

5. **betraying** (a secret)
   a) giving away
   b) hiding
   c) denying
   d) harming

6. **native**
   a) person visiting a particular place
   b) person who has brought fame to
      a particular place
   c) person born or raised in a
      particular place
   d) newcomer to a particular place

7. **ceased**
   a) begun
   b) stopped
   c) continued
   d) re-started

8. **resent**
   a) remember
   b) recount
   c) feel perplexed about
   d) feel bitter about

9. **conversion** (to the Faith)
   a) act of becoming a Catholic
   b) act of becoming a religious
   c) act of becoming a priest
   d) act of becoming a bishop

10. **ordination**
    a) ceremony making one a Catholic
    b) ceremony making one a religious
    c) ceremony making one a priest
    d) ceremony making one a bishop

11. **prejudice**
    a) unfair preconceived opinion
    b) feeling of dislike
    c) unfair religous or political power
    d) false prediction or prophecy

12. **aversion**
    a) extreme selfishness
    b) extreme suspicion
    c) strong fear
    d) strong dislike

13. **Count**
    a) a kind of businessman
    b) a kind of nobleman
    c) a kind of elected official
    d) a kind of military officer

14. **ardent**
    a) serious, hard-working
    b) joyful, happy
    c) fervent, enthusiastic
    d) extraordinary, remarkable

15. convert
  a) someone who has become a Catholic
  b) someone who has become a religious
  c) someone planning to become a Catholic
  d) someone planning to become a religious

16. nevertheless
  a) in spite of that
  b) because of that
  c) after that
  d) with that in mind

17. steadfastly
  a) easily
  b) indifferently
  c) uninterruptedly
  d) interestedly

18. spied
  a) paid attention to
  b) inspected
  c) glanced at
  d) caught sight of

19. dumbfounded
  a) amazed
  b) horrified
  c) joyful
  d) exhilarated

20. bounds
  a) rhythms
  b) rhymes
  c) limits
  d) gaps

The Rays

Chapter 16

Perfect Score: 100   Score: _____

1. marvel
  a) ponder
  b) rejoice
  c) be devoted
  d) be amazed

2. seminary
  a) school that trains men to become religious
  b) school that trains men to become priests
  c) school in which men and women study theology
  d) school in which non-Catholics learn how to become Catholics

3. race
  a) people
  b) history
  c) religion
  d) temple

4. aspect
  a) teaching, doctrine
  b) petition, request
  c) part, side
  d) attraction, benefit

5. longingly
  a) with gratitude
  b) with desire
  c) with anxiety
  d) with joy

6. concerning
  a) due to
  b) after
  c) because of
  d) relating to

7. **pondered**
   a) understood
   b) decided on
   c) realized
   d) reflected upon

8. **torrents**
   a) gushing streams
   b) trickling droplets
   c) steady flows
   d) gradual streams

9. **reference**
   a) announcement
   b) definition
   c) mention
   d) discussion

10. **afterthought**
    a) idea that occurred later
    b) idea that was discussed later
    c) less important idea
    d) creative idea

11. **swelled** (literal meaning)
    a) shrank or decreased
    b) grew or increased
    c) rose higher
    d) developed

12. **era**
    a) month
    b) year
    c) specific date in history
    d) period of time

13. **obscure**
    a) not observant
    b) little known
    c) not devout
    d) well known

14. **canonically**
    a) pertaining to an association
    b) according to the law of the nation
    c) according to Church law
    d) pertaining to lay people

15. **granted**
    a) officially displayed
    b) officially given
    c) officially agreed
    d) officially announced

16. **doctrine**
    a) teaching
    b) law
    c) devotion
    d) rule

17. **Article of Faith**
    a) lesson that must be learned
    b) moral law that must be obeyed
    c) truth that must be believed
    d) statement that must be publicized

18. **nineteenth century**
    a) the years from 1701-1800
    b) the years from 1801-1900
    c) the years from 1901-2000
    d) the years from 2001-2100

19. **witnessing**
    a) analyzing
    b) seeing
    c) believing
    d) celebrating

20. **untold**
    a) unprepared
    b) countless
    c) unnoticed
    d) universal

"The Streets Will
Run with Blood"

Chapter 17

Text
Pages
81-85

Perfect Score: 100   **Score:** _____

1. feeble
   a) miserable
   b) ugly
   c) slow
   d) weak

2. overtook
   a) hurt
   b) upset
   c) caught up with
   d) took advantage of

3. vicious
   a) very immoral
   b) greedy for wealth
   c) deceitful, dishonest
   d) greedy for power

4. in cold blood
   a) without preparation or foresight
   b) without mercy or emotion
   c) without good cause
   d) without firearms

5. desecrated
   a) destroyed
   b) treated with grave disrespect
   c) closed down
   d) bombed or set on fire

6. convulsed (literal meaning)
   a) totally destroyed
   b) seriously warned
   c) caused to suffer
   d) violently shaken

7. calamities
   a) obstacles
   b) catastrophes
   c) problems
   d) incidents

8. despised
   a) disdained and looked down upon
   b) destroyed or severely damaged
   c) treated with a lukewarm attitude
   d) abandoned, forsaken

9. trodden
   a) trampled
   b) lowered
   c) mocked
   d) destroyed

10. showered upon
   a) given wisely to
   b) given prudently to
   c) given in abundance to
   d) given with reluctance to

11. posts
   a) dangerous places
   b) assigned stations
   c) convents
   d) hospitals or infirmaries

12. object to
   a) block, prevent
   b) protest, disapprove of
   c) ignore, refuse to notice
   d) assist, facilitate

13. haven
   a) place of recreation
   b) place of work
   c) place of prayer
   d) place of safety

14. mob
   a) large group of protestors
   b) persistent, determined crowd
   c) large, disorderly crowd
   d) firing squad

15. falter
   a) increase
   b) waver
   c) vanish
   d) die

16. verdict
   a) judgment, decision
   b) law, rule
   c) idea, concept
   d) order, command

17. rebels
   a) persons who have strong political opinions
   b) police officers of the established government
   c) persons who take up arms against their government
   d) persons who exercise violence toward others

18. fortress
   a) government headquarters
   b) hiding place
   c) heavily defended place
   d) place where weapons are made

19. boasted
   a) announced
   b) warned
   c) threatened
   d) bragged

20. ruthless
   a) merciless, cruel
   b) conceited, vain
   c) arrogant, prideful
   d) greedy, selfish

A New Request
from Our Lady

A Disappointing
Trip

Chapters 18, 19

Text
Pages
86-94

Perfect Score: 100   Score: _____

1. exile
   a) desired separation from one's home or country
   b) unexpected separation from one's home or country
   c) forced separation from one's home or country
   d) voluntary separation from one's home or country

2. innocent
   a) fearless
   b) homeless
   c) blameless
   d) helpless

3. mingled with
   a) providing a background for
   b) intermixed with
   c) overcoming
   d) added to

4. namely
   a) despite the fact
   b) on account of the fact
   c) that is to say
   d) indeed, truly

5. strain
   a) stress
   b) situation
   c) difficulty
   d) question

6. recreation

a) activity done for enjoyment or relaxation
b) activity done out of a sense of duty or responsibility
c) activity done because it is expected
d) activity done without good reason

7. labor

a) farming
b) duty
c) burden
d) work

8. poultry

a) any farm animals
b) animals raised for meat and milk
c) birds raised for meat and eggs
d) animals raised for meat and wool

9. consultations

a) rumors
b) assumptions
c) discussions
d) suggestions

10. rheumatism

a) disorder characterized by difficulty in breathing
b) disorder characterized by headaches
c) disorder characterized by difficulties in sleeping
d) disorder characterized by pain and stiffness

11. ventured

a) decided
b) dared
c) started
d) agreed

---

12. destination

a) place to which one is going
b) place where one makes a rest stop
c) destiny
d) hotel

13. transferred

a) promoted, moved up to a higher status
b) demoted, reduced to a lower status
c) moved, re-assigned
d) retired

14. parlor

a) lobby, foyer
b) office, study
c) dining room, refectory
d) room for receiving visitors

15. a trifle

a) a little
b) very
c) obviously
d) definitely

16. valiant

a) visible, obvious
b) strong, heroic
c) steady, uninterrupted
d) virtuous, moral

17. missionary

a) person sent to find out information
b) person sent to do religious work
c) person sent to bring back supplies
d) person sent on retreat

18. fatigue

a) weariness
b) sorrow
c) disappointment
d) hopelessness

19. fulfill

a) begin, initiate
b) obey, submit to
c) respect, revere
d) carry out, accomplish

20. privileged

a) pious
b) unknown
c) favored
d) important

VOCABULARY QUIZ WORKBOOK

Sister Catherine Breaks
Her Long Silence

Sister Catherine's
Last Request

Chapters 20, 21

Text
Pages
95-106

Perfect Score: 100   **Score:** _____

1. **indulgently**
   a) in a spirit of encouraging someone
   b) in a spirit of reprimanding someone
   c) in a spirit of giving in to someone's desires
   d) in a spirit of resisting someone's desires

2. **appointed**
   a) desired, longed for
   b) designated
   c) suggested
   d) approved

3. **stupefied**
   a) expectant
   b) annoyed
   c) respectful
   d) astonished

4. **awed**
   a) filled with joy and gladness
   b) filled with disappointment or dismay
   c) filled with relief
   d) filled with respect and wonderment

5. **customary**
   a) habitual
   b) common-sense
   c) strong
   d) helpful

6. **practicality**
   a) sense of authority
   b) piety and devotion
   c) common-sense approach
   d) understanding of religious matters

7. **proceeding**
   a) going forth
   b) shining
   c) rising, ascending
   d) descending

8. **graces**
   a) Bibles and Rosaries
   b) prayers to the Saints
   c) supernatural merits
   d) supernatural helps from God

9. **blessings**
   a) food and shelter
   b) Sacraments
   c) sacramentals
   d) any gifts from God

10. **dawn**
    a) first light of morning
    b) last light of evening
    c) light of a solar eclipse
    d) light of a lunar eclipse

11. **hastily**
    a) graciously
    b) surprisingly
    c) hurriedly
    d) with surprise

12. **revelation**
  a) deep understanding
  b) bad news
  c) information made known
  d) wonderful announcement

13. **procuring**
  a) purchasing
  b) obtaining
  c) investigating
  d) seeking

14. **capture**
  a) meditate upon
  b) record in lasting form
  c) understand completely
  d) appreciate fully

15. **inspiring**
  a) thought-provoking
  b) instructive, educational
  c) tastefully done, artistic
  d) stirring, uplifting

16. **remark**
  a) explanation
  b) rumor
  c) comment
  d) recommendation

17. **confined**
  a) restricted
  b) resigned
  c) connected
  d) ordered

18. **worn**
  a) old
  b) wearied
  c) ill
  d) disabled

19. **acquaintance**
  a) care
  b) hometown
  c) familiarity
  d) area

20. **murmured**
  a) said softly
  b) said quickly
  c) said happily
  d) said with emphasis

Instructions: Circle the letter of the answer which best matches the meaning of the vocabulary word.

A Fool or a Saint?

Chapter 1

Text
Pages
1-5

Perfect Score: 100

Score: _____

1. peered
a) scowled menacingly
b) peeked curiously
c) analyzed carefully
d) pointed

2. striding
a) running
b) jogging
c) walking with long steps
d) walking with short steps

3. briskly
a) energetically
b) desperately
c) nervously
d) lazily

4. hearth
a) heater, stove
b) floor of a fireplace
c) pile of firewood
d) parlor, visiting room

5. moodily
a) in a lively, interested manner
b) in an angry or argumentative manner
c) in a crude, coarse manner
d) in a gloomy or absent-minded manner

6. heedless of
a) not paying attention to
b) annoyed by
c) angry about
d) unable to hear

7. on the threshold
a) in the hallway
b) in the lobby
c) in the doorway
d) by the fireplace

8. sheaf
a) box
b) group
c) bundle
d) envelope

9. wryly
a) with sparkling eyes
b) with eyes looking misty
c) with a blank look on one's face
d) with a one-sided smile

10. mortified
a) in the habit of practicing self-denial
b) in the habit of living a studious life
c) in the habit of living a self-indulgent life
d) in the habit of praying regularly

11. shabby
 a) old
 b) unclean, unwashed
 c) antiquated, outdated
 d) worn, dingy

12. hangings
 a) rare paintings
 b) decorations hung on walls
 c) potted plants fixed to the walls
 d) lights hung from ceilings

13. approaching
 a) upcoming
 b) dreaded
 c) recent
 d) expected

14. interview
 a) announcement
 b) intervention
 c) conference
 d) assignment

15. timidly
 a) quietly, silently
 b) with great composure
 c) indifferently
 d) fearfully, not courageously

16. the latter
 a) the earlier one mentioned
 b) the later one mentioned
 c) the higher-ranking one mentioned
 d) the lower-ranking one mentioned

17. frankly
 a) with all due respect
 b) honestly, forthrightly
 c) without offense
 d) without respect

18. prudent
 a) knowledgeable, learned
 b) pious, devout
 c) generous, unselfish
 d) wise, careful

19. repulsive
 a) political
 b) unjust
 c) unnecessary
 d) revolting

20. remorseful
 a) regretful
 b) forgetful
 c) embarrassed
 d) outraged

A Slave

Chapter 2

Perfect Score: 100

Score: _____

1. board
 a) place to sleep
 b) place to work
 c) daily schedule
 d) daily meals

2. enveloped
 a) surrounded
 b) encumbered
 c) disguised
 d) adorned

3. accommodated
 a) registered, enlisted
 b) provided for
 c) ignored
 d) treated with contempt

4. quarters
 a) a place to study
 b) a place to live
 c) a place to eat
 d) a place to work

5. declined
a) accepted
b) satisfied
c) refused
d) agreed to

6. lodgers
a) residents
b) beggars
c) poor persons
d) patients

7. petitioned
a) demanded as a group
b) suggested as a group
c) considered as a group
d) requested as a group

8. chaplain
a) priest who is sent to foreign missions
b) priest who ministers at a parish
c) priest who ministers at a cathedral
d) priest who ministers at an institution

9. reflected
a) rejoiced
b) thought
c) decided
d) guessed

10. twilight
a) moonlight
b) light of dawn or dusk
c) light of a solar eclipse
d) daylight on a cloudy day

11. sizeable
a) fairly large
b) immeasureable
c) fairly small
d) of a specific size

12. feeble
a) small
b) disturbed
c) weak
d) disabled

13. garbed
a) covered
b) clothed
c) in uniform
d) disguised

14. homespun
a) polyester cloth
b) plain-weave cloth
c) uniform
d) religious habit

15. wan
a) pale
b) nervous
c) patient
d) expectant

16. matron
a) man in charge of domestic affairs
b) woman in charge of domestic affairs
c) man in charge of financial planning
d) woman in charge of financial planning

17. made the acquaintance of
a) became partners with
b) visited
c) became friends with
d) met

18. retiring
a) eating supper
b) going to bed
c) praying evening prayers
d) saying goodbye

19. heed
a) understanding
b) displeasure
c) attention
d) surprise

20. merit
a) spiritual value
b) spiritual mortification
c) spiritual effort
d) spiritual aid

Trouble with the
Poorhouse Staff

Chapter 3

Text
Pages
10-15

Perfect Score: 100   Score: _____

1. **zeal**
   a) holy enthusiasm
   b) holy joy
   c) holy wisdom
   d) holy generosity

2. **a score**
   a) 10
   b) 12
   c) 20
   d) 100

3. **formerly**
   a) usually
   b) unsatisfactorily
   c) previously
   d) naturally

4. **plight**
   a) complaint
   b) distressing condition
   c) complicated problem
   d) desperate request

5. **ample**
   a) small and delicate
   b) heavy, overburdened
   c) strong, sturdy
   d) large and roomy

6. **indignantly**
   a) with dismay and discouragement
   b) with anger and disapproval
   c) with pride and arrogance
   d) with puzzlement and confusion

7. **restrained**
   a) decided against
   b) held back
   c) rethought
   d) expressed

8. **shiftless**
   a) heartless
   b) deceitful
   c) bad
   d) lazy

9. **lot**
   a) effort
   b) effect
   c) group
   d) arrangement

10. **downright**
    a) seemingly
    b) thoroughly
    c) fairly
    d) almost

11. **dryly**
    a) in an indignant manner
    b) in an authoritative manner
    c) in a matter-of-fact manner
    d) in a frustrated manner

12. **allotted**
    a) donated
    b) added
    c) contributed
    d) assigned

13. **shrewd**
    a) clever in practical affairs
    b) obnoxious in practical affairs
    c) dishonest in practical affairs
    d) unpleasant in practical affairs

14. **composure**
    a) self-esteem
    b) self-possession
    c) rudeness
    d) point of view

15. wretches

    a) homeless people

    b) miserable people

    c) bad people

    d) lazy people

16. on no account

    a) not without good reason

    b) not without a grave circumstance

    c) only under extreme conditions

    d) under no circumstances

17. remedy

    a) discourage

    b) realize

    c) correct

    d) better understand

18. graciousness

    a) enthusiasm

    b) eagerness

    c) kindliness

    d) joyfulness

19. the afflicted

    a) irreligious people

    b) distressed people

    c) confused people

    d) wicked people

20. harassed

    a) hopeless

    b) confused

    c) angry

    d) strained

Father Grignion
Disappears

Father Grignion's
Advice

Chapters 4, 5

Text
Pages
16-25

Perfect Score: 100   Score: _____

1. ventured

    a) realized

    b) decided

    c) dared

    d) learned

2. trial

    a) circumstance

    b) distraction

    c) surprise

    d) difficulty

3. intervals

    a) stopping places

    b) pre-announced places

    c) 4-week periods

    d) spaces of time

4. devout

    a) virtuous, moral

    b) hard-working, diligent

    c) pious, religious

    d) honest, sincere

5. incredulously

    a) in an unbelieving manner

    b) in a typical manner

    c) in a concerned manner

    d) in a flustered manner

6. reverent

    a) spiritual

    b) prayerful

    c) respectful

    d) faithful

7. uncooperatively

    a) forcefully, aggressively

    b) unhelpfully, balkily

    c) shyly, timidly

    d) confusedly, perplexedly

8. chisel

    a) tool used for melting materials

    b) tool used for building

    c) tool used for moving stone

    d) tool used for carving stone

9. **emphatically**
   a) sincerely
   b) eagerly
   c) negatively
   d) forcefully

10. **pondering**
    a) hesitating over
    b) believing confidently
    c) thinking deeply about
    d) remembering clearly

11. **forsaken**
    a) distressed
    b) abandoned
    c) confused
    d) sorrowful

----

12. **reproach**
    a) blame
    b) advice
    c) discouragement
    d) explanation

13. **claim**
    a) punish
    b) give
    c) find
    d) demand

14. **on the wane**
    a) growing weaker
    b) posing a challenge
    c) growing stronger
    d) on the rampage

15. **speculation**
    a) conjecture, theorizing
    b) planning, strategizing
    c) blame, judgment
    d) suspicion, distrust

16. **persecuted**
    a) misjudged
    b) disagreed with
    c) treated unjustly
    d) treated thoughtlessly

17. **anxiety**
    a) preparation
    b) desire
    c) illness
    d) worry

18. **relate**
    a) solve
    b) tell
    c) figure out
    d) confess

19. **shifted**
    a) looked up
    b) turned around
    c) changed positions
    d) jerked up

20. **litany**
    a) prayer to Our Lady prayed after the Rosary
    b) prayer consisting of Scriptural quotations
    c) prayer of contrition and reparation
    d) prayer invoking someone by a list of titles

Consecration to Mary

Preparing and
More Preparing

Chapters 6, 7

Text
Pages
26-36

Perfect Score: 100　　　　　　　　　　　　　　**Score:** _____

1. disregarded
a) hated
b) purposely ignored
c) obeyed under protest
d) argued against

2. invalids
a) persons who live at an institution
b) persons who have no money
c) persons chronically ill or disabled
d) persons undergoing physical therapy

3. scandalized
a) shocked
b) slandered
c) indifferent
d) frightened

4. impulsively
a) thoughtfully
b) suddenly
c) hesitantly
d) trustingly

- -

5. mad
a) stupid
b) obnoxious
c) bothersome
d) insane

6. bluntly
a) disappointedly, sadly
b) with annoyance
c) diplomatically or subtly
d) without subtlety

7. queer
a) creative
b) strange
c) unpopular
d) harmful

8. henceforth
a) therefore
b) from now on
c) heretofore
d) thence

9. appeal to
a) attract, impress
b) educate, inform
c) make indifferent
d) alienate

10. border on
a) have an effect on
b) result from
c) verge on
d) be in the habit of

11. mistress
a) maiden
b) woman who has authority or ownership
c) saintly woman
d) patroness

12. goods
a) possessions
b) results
c) origins
d) slavery

13. untold
a) countless
b) spiritual
c) particular
d) several

14. concerning
   a) discussing
   b) relating to
   c) avoiding
   d) ignoring

15. misled
   a) impatient
   b) deceived
   c) misunderstood
   d) discouraged

16. grasping
   a) understanding
   b) accepting
   c) believing
   d) learning

17. stupendous
   a) causing great happiness
   b) interesting, arousing curiosity
   c) devout, religious
   d) marvelous, awesome

18. stifling
   a) facing
   b) suppressing
   c) accepting
   d) ignoring

19. submissively
   a) uncaringly
   b) sadly
   c) compliantly
   d) shyly

20. proceeded to
   a) offered to
   b) decided to
   c) started to
   d) tried to

Ready at Last   # Chapter 8   Text Pages 37-40

Perfect Score: 100   Score: _____

1. ends
   a) methods
   b) goals
   c) efforts
   d) attitudes

2. contrition
   a) examination of conscience
   b) mercy
   c) sorrow for sin, repentance
   d) pardon, forgiveness of sin

3. detachment from
   a) freeing oneself from
   b) improvement of one's position in
   c) interest in
   d) renewal of one's relationship to

4. objective
   a) effect
   b) interest
   c) goal
   d) method

5. fashion
   a) advantage
   b) desire
   c) effort
   d) way

6. conceiving (thoughts, desires)
   a) analyzing, studying
   b) obeying, carrying out
   c) desiring, wanting
   d) perceiving, formulating

7. **consoled**
   a) comforted
   b) depressed
   c) surprised
   d) delighted

8. **composed**
   a) revealed
   b) changed
   c) authored
   d) published

9. **consisted of**
   a) ended with
   b) put emphasis on
   c) began with
   d) was made up of

10. **securing**
    a) affecting
    b) obtaining
    c) promising
    d) creating

11. **applied oneself**
    a) exerted effort
    b) received guidance
    c) felt desires
    d) took direction

12. **recitation**
    a) saying something improvised
    b) repeating a set formula
    c) meditation
    d) saying something holy

13. **groundless**
    a) without sincerity
    b) without good reasons
    c) without a good attitude
    d) without guidance

14. **humility**
    a) virtue of thinking that one is nothing at all
    b) virtue of realizing that one is nothing without God
    c) virtue of thinking that one has less talent than everyone else
    d) virtue of believing that one is worthless

15. **apt**
    a) eager
    b) strong
    c) weak
    d) inclined

16. **profit**
    a) benefit
    b) demonstrate
    c) desire
    d) prove

17. **repel** (literal meaning)
    a) push out
    b) push away
    c) put on
    d) put away

18. **vigorously**
    a) reassuringly
    b) confidently
    c) slowly
    d) energetically

19. **union with**
    a) desire for
    b) joining to
    c) devotion to
    d) imitation of

20. **dependence**
    a) reliance
    b) acceptance
    c) influence
    d) imitation

Mary Louise's
Vocation

Chapter 9

Text
Pages
41-46

Perfect Score: 100   Score: _____

1. **glimpsed**
   a) thoroughly understood
   b) hoped for and dreamed about
   c) briefly caught sight of
   d) joyfully discovered

2. **at the expense of**
   a) paid for by
   b) costing much money
   c) costing little money
   d) paying the bills

3. **dowry**
   a) sum of money required for entering
      some convents
   b) diploma required for entering some
      convents
   c) training required for entering some
      convents
   d) recommendation required for
      entering some convents

4. **friar**
   a) priest teaching at a seminary
   b) priest who serves the poor
   c) holy man
   d) man belonging to a religious order

5. **secular**
   a) not serving at a cathedral
   b) not belonging to a religious order
   c) not serving in a parish
   d) not serving in the foreign missions

6. **disconsolately**
   a) angrily
   b) anxiously
   c) dejectedly
   d) incoherently

7. **absence**
   a) period of being present
   b) period of not being present
   c) period of being busy
   d) period of being on a mission

8. **province**
   a) capital of a country
   b) city of a country
   c) border of a country
   d) region of a country

9. **incredible** (literal meaning)
   a) undeserved
   b) unaccustomed
   c) unrecognized
   d) unbelievable

10. **observed**
    a) announced
    b) decided
    c) remarked
    d) reassured

11. **mildly**
    a) thoughtfully
    b) interestedly
    c) helpfully
    d) gently

12. **remarked**
    a) announced
    b) reasoned
    c) commented
    d) discussed

13. **indifferently**
    a) in an impressive manner
    b) in an uncaring manner
    c) in a responsible manner
    d) in a sensitive manner

14. obtained
   a) persuaded
   b) firmly established
   c) found, discovered
   d) gained possession of

15. dismay
   a) relief and satisfaction
   b) great annoyance, irritation
   c) disinterest, lack of concern
   d) sudden and severe disappointment

16. consent
   a) knowledge
   b) approval
   c) protection
   d) assistance

17. winced
   a) flinched
   b) nodded
   c) frowned
   d) wept

18. dubiously
   a) kindly
   b) decisively
   c) sternly
   d) doubtfully

19. obstacles
   a) obligations
   b) attitudes
   c) accommodations
   d) barriers

20. resolutely
   a) obediently
   b) faithfully
   c) determinedly
   d) hesitatingly

| Mary Louise's New Life | # Chapter 10 | Text Pages 47-50 |

Perfect Score: 100   Score: _____

1. informing
   a) scolding
   b) discouraging
   c) promising
   d) telling

2. prominent
   a) well known and important
   b) rich and comfortable
   c) cheerful and well-liked
   d) powerful in the government

3. persevere
   a) do penance
   b) have patience
   c) preserve
   d) persist

4. meager
   a) unappetizing
   b) scanty
   c) plain
   d) not nutritious

5. accommodations
   a) responsibilities
   b) housing
   c) clothing
   d) mortifications

6. companionship
   a) confidence
   b) assistance
   c) association
   d) charity

7. official
   a) authorized
   b) important
   c) honorable
   d) high-ranking

8. capacity
   a) room
   b) position
   c) time
   d) schedule

9. taken aback
   a) worried
   b) saddened
   c) discouraged
   d) surprised

10. brusqueness
   a) abruptness
   b) anger
   c) indifference
   d) deceitfulness

11. case
   a) disagreement
   b) problem
   c) position
   d) challenge

12. persisted
   a) argued
   b) persevered
   c) asked
   d) pestered

13. renewed
   a) obvious
   b) partial
   c) fixed
   d) revived

14. bashfully
   a) kindly
   b) shyly
   c) sympathetically
   d) earnestly

15. objections
   a) explanations
   b) problems
   c) protests
   d) opinions

16. meditation
   a) mental prayer
   b) vocal prayer
   c) religious study
   d) retreat

17. recreation
   a) change
   b) exercise
   c) relaxation
   d) work

18. undismayed
   a) not discouraged
   b) not caring
   c) not understanding
   d) not concerned

19. erected
   a) put up
   b) displayed
   c) taken down
   d) positioned

20. misgivings
   a) grudges
   b) hesitations
   c) regrets
   d) arguments

Chapter 11

Perfect Score: 100   **Score:** _____

1. **paupers**
   a) diseased persons
   b) criminals
   c) despised persons
   d) poor persons

2. **hastened**
   a) hurried
   b) decided
   c) started
   d) attempted

3. **suitable**
   a) desirable
   b) comfortable
   c) enjoyable
   d) appropriate

4. **pang**
   a) slowly developing pain or anguish
   b) sudden pain or anguish
   c) feeling of anger or irritation
   d) firm decision

5. **grief**
   a) confusion
   b) sorrow
   c) exasperation
   d) anger

6. **absently**
   a) distractedly
   b) purposely
   c) deliberately
   d) curiously

7. **bewilderment**
   a) surprise, shock
   b) childlike obedience
   c) complete puzzlement
   d) trusting acceptance

8. **orphanage**
   a) home for handicapped children
   b) home for delinquent children
   c) home for children without parents
   d) home for children without grandparents

9. **roused**
   a) reminded
   b) forced
   c) distracted
   d) stirred

10. **preoccupation**
    a) state of being absorbed in thought
    b) state of being completely confused
    c) state of being curious
    d) state of being hurt or anguished

11. **reference**
    a) effort
    b) instruction
    c) imitation
    d) mention

12. **nevertheless**
    a) in addition to that
    b) in spite of that
    c) actually
    d) because of that

13. **opposition**
    a) reaction
    b) attitude
    c) resistance
    d) strangeness

14. **congregation**
    a) career
    b) community
    c) devotion
    d) way of life

15. Purification
a) feast day also known as The Nativity
b) feast day also known as Candlemas Day
c) feast day also known as Michaelmas Day
d) feast day also known as Whitsunday

16. incidentally
a) in the meantime
b) more importantly
c) by the way
d) if there is time

17. gaze
a) stare
b) glance
c) peek
d) inspect

18. cloistered
a) underground
b) devoted to some particular work
c) secluded from the world
d) consecrated

19. seldom
a) never
b) somewhat
c) sometimes
d) rarely

20. sanctified
a) made bearable
b) merited
c) made holy
d) sacrificed

Shock Waves
from Jansenism

Chapter 12

Text
Pages
56-60

Perfect Score: 100

Score: _____

1. supposing
a) dreading
b) realizing
c) discovering
d) assuming

2. stir
a) commotion
b) rumor
c) riot
d) misunderstanding

3. gaping
a) inspecting and analyzing
b) staring with open mouth
c) curiously listening
d) mocking or smirking

4. (necks) craned
a) appeared
b) bobbed
c) ducked
d) stretched

5. harrowing
a) pitiful
b) angering
c) tormenting
d) disappointing

6. accompanied
a) led
b) followed
c) assisted
d) gone along with

7. baneful
a) relieved, grateful
b) victorious, triumphant
c) distressed, worried
d) negative, disapproving

8. alms
a) job earning
b) donation to the poor
c) loan
d) stolen money

VOCABULARY QUIZ WORKBOOK

9. sternly
  a) persuasively
  b) severely
  c) angrily
  d) calmly

10. slighting
  a) disdainful
  b) clever
  c) dishonest
  d) unforgiveable

11. zealous
  a) holy
  b) well-meaning
  c) sincere
  d) fervent

12. aghast
  a) surprised
  b) grieved
  c) horrified
  d) bothered

13. had retracted
  a) had renewed
  b) had taken back
  c) had publicized
  d) had ignored

14. condemned
  a) declared to be wrong
  b) analyzed thoroughly
  c) publicized widely
  d) suspected of error

15. circulation
  a) distribution
  b) authorization
  c) prohibition
  d) completion

16. publicity
  a) scholarship
  b) deception
  c) intensity
  d) attention

17. enlighten
  a) give hope to
  b) give understanding to
  c) give comfort to
  d) give humility to

18. welfare
  a) welcome
  b) freedom
  c) well-being
  d) poverty

19. at stake
  a) in competition
  b) at risk
  c) prohibited
  d) outlawed

20. faltered
  a) said with sorrow
  b) said with uncertainty
  c) demanded
  d) inquired

Searching for
God's Will

Chapter 13

Text
Pages
61-67

Perfect Score: 100   Score: _____

1. ambition
  a) ability
  b) desire
  c) pastime
  d) work

2. New France
  a) New Orleans in pioneer days
  b) New England in pioneer days
  c) Canada in pioneer days
  d) Virginia in pioneer days

3. ruefully
   a) regretfully
   b) jealously
   c) happily
   d) determinedly

4. mission (parish mission)
   a) a series of special church services
      to renew the spiritual life of the
      faithful
   b) a series of religion classes taught by
      a priest to educate the faithful
   c) a series of sermons and collections
      of money for the Church in foreign
      lands
   d) a series of fundraising activities in
      and for a parish

5. districts
   a) meeting halls
   b) fields, farmlands
   c) schoolhouses
   d) regions, sections

6. cherished
   a) treasured
   b) respected
   c) admired
   d) appreciated

7. influential
   a) scholarly
   b) familiar
   c) powerful
   d) respectable

8. bore (past tense of bear)
   a) challenged
   b) fought
   c) ignored
   d) endured

9. economically
   a) politically
   b) extravagantly
   c) cost-effectively
   d) generously

10. campaign
   a) single aggressive activity aimed at
      a specific purpose
   b) series of aggressive activities aimed
      at a specific purpose
   c) series of enjoyable activities for the
      purpose of relaxation
   d) series of purposeless activities

11. slander
   a) false charges that damage another's
      reputation
   b) true statements that damage
      another's reputation
   c) idle chatter about another
   d) lawsuits against another

12. curt
   a) rudely brief
   b) courteous, polite
   c) firm but kind
   d) apologetic

13. dismissal
   a) transfer to another location
   b) notification of upcoming punishment
   c) removal from one's position
   d) loss of reputation

14. dilapidated
   a) abandoned, unused
   b) in partial ruin
   c) uncleaned, filthy
   d) old or ancient

15. landlord
   a) person who takes in the poor for free
   b) merchant
   c) person who rents out housing
   d) banker

16. ignorant
   a) careless
   b) envious
   c) unconcerned
   d) unknowing

17. idleness
   a) absence of money
   b) absence of comfort
   c) absence of rest
   d) absence of activity

18. found
   a) establish
   b) discover
   c) publicize
   d) substitute

19. duration
   a) necessity
   b) continuation
   c) insistence
   d) expectation

20. encountered
   a) saw
   b) met
   c) discovered
   d) was discovered by

| "Father, Please Come Back!" | **Chapter 14** | Text Pages 68-72 |

Perfect Score: 100   Score: _____

1. lofty
   a) difficult to climb
   b) high
   c) obscure
   d) distant

2. grim
   a) very serious, cheerless
   b) very unhelpful, indifferent
   c) very sorrowful, mournful
   d) very regretful, remorseful

3. scandal
   a) uncertain situation
   b) problematic situation
   c) uncontrollable situation
   d) disgraceful situation

4. threadbare
   a) very worn
   b) very faded
   c) very old
   d) very out-of-style

5. headway
   a) damage
   b) corruption
   c) progress
   d) change

6. recalling
   a) pondering
   b) remembering
   c) analyzing
   d) learning from

7. grievance
   a) fact
   b) complaint
   c) situation
   d) argument

8. hermits
   a) religious brothers who work in parishes
   b) religious brothers who work at a cathedral
   c) religious brothers who spend much time assisting the poor
   d) religious brothers who spend much time in solitude

9. inconsiderate
   a) forgetful
   b) lazy, slothful
   c) neglectful of one's duties
   d) thoughtless toward others

10. ill-tempered
   a) irritable
   b) slothful
   c) malicious
   d) depressed

11. repugnant
   a) difficult
   b) distasteful
   c) challenging
   d) impossible

12. make light of
   a) be afraid of
   b) be overwhelmed by
   c) pay too much attention to, overreact to
   d) place little importance on

13. minimize
   a) treat as if unimportant
   b) pay too much attention to
   c) treat as horrifying
   d) treat as offensive

14. bearing fruit
   a) causing changes
   b) making adjustments
   c) making peace
   d) having good results

15. to the letter
   a) satisfactorily
   b) noticeably
   c) exactly
   d) successfully

16. vice
   a) problem
   b) sinful habit
   c) complaint
   d) trial, temptation

17. abode
   a) dwelling place
   b) hidden place
   c) favorite place
   d) place of prayer

18. close (noun)
   a) climax
   b) planning stage
   c) beginning
   d) conclusion

19. had disbanded
   a) had quit and refused to continue
   b) had broken up and separated
   c) had become confused
   d) had been destroyed

20. lot
   a) environment, surroundings
   b) mood, attitude
   c) condition in life
   d) daily routine

Sister Mary
Louise's Decision

Chapter 15

Text
Pages
73-79

Perfect Score: 100   Score: _____

1. piety
a) serious nature
b) sense of duty
c) religious knowledge
d) religious devotion

2. indulgently
a) amusedly
b) innocently
c) compliantly
d) enthusiastically

3. disdain
a) disbelief
b) scorn
c) dismay
d) amusement

4. mock
a) simulated
b) secret
c) utter
d) disguised

5. air
a) hymn
b) love song
c) tune
d) harmony

6. fancy
a) attention
b) curiosity
c) liking
d) habit

7. gay
a) cheerful
b) popular
c) famous
d) recent

8. obligingly
a) with great eagerness
b) promptly
c) in a matter-of-fact manner
d) as a favor to someone

9. trial
a) consideration
b) tryout
c) favorable view
d) decision

10. departure
a) act of saying farewell
b) act of leaving
c) act of mounting a horse
d) act of getting into a carriage

11. choicest
a) most interesting
b) most appreciated
c) spiritual
d) best

12. dignity
a) routine
b) responsibility
c) decorum
d) obedience

13. notions
a) meditations
b) actions
c) ideas
d) objections

14. **safeguard**
   a) protect
   b) satisfy
   c) nurture
   d) fight for

15. **prejudice**
   a) opposition based on good reasons
   b) opposition based on preconceived opinion
   c) lies and deceit used against someone
   d) political power used against someone

16. **abandon**
   a) forget
   b) give up
   c) ignore
   d) reject

17. **indignation**
   a) hurt feelings
   b) annoyance
   c) anger
   d) dissatisfaction

18. **malicious**
   a) acting like busybodies
   b) acting like babies
   c) having misdirected good intentions
   d) having bad will

19. **compelled**
   a) persuaded
   b) tricked
   c) forced
   d) encouraged

20. **serenely**
   a) peacefully
   b) reassuringly
   c) determinedly
   d) quietly

Preaching in
the Streets

The Young
Stranger

Chapters 16, 17

Text
Pages
80-89

Perfect Score: 100

Score: _____

1. **conflicting**
   a) opposing
   b) interesting
   c) aggravating
   d) confusing

2. **deplored**
   a) strongly resisted
   b) despised
   c) discouraged
   d) strongly regretted

3. **a trifle**
   a) very
   b) strangely
   c) a little
   d) considerably

4. **adjoining**
   a) surrounding
   b) included with
   c) connected with
   d) in the vicinity of

5. outlying
   a) on the outskirts
   b) out of sight
   c) outlawed
   d) centrally located

6. dire
   a) undeniable
   b) reckless
   c) desperate
   d) serious

7. converts
   a) persons who have changed to
      a better way of life
   b) persons who have listened to
      sermons with great attention
   c) persons who contribute money to
      a religious work
   d) persons who contribute time and
      energy to a religious work

8. stirring
   a) sincere
   b) interesting
   c) revealing
   d) moving

9. flourished
   a) persisted
   b) thrived
   c) triumphed
   d) developed

10. maintain
   a) preserve
   b) beautify
   c) organize
   d) supervise

11. modest (sum)
   a) very small, meager
   b) very large, generous
   c) fair, just
   d) fairly small, moderate

12. sum
   a) bargain price
   b) financial agreement
   c) amount of money
   d) trade, barter

13. appeal
   a) impressiveness
   b) dignity
   c) attractiveness
   d) familiarity

- -

14. suburb
   a) community adjacent to a city
   b) community out in the country
   c) community in the middle of a city
   d) poor community, slum

15. vastly
   a) obviously
   b) necessarily
   c) immensely
   d) somewhat

16. akin to
   a) inspired by
   b) similar to
   c) challenged by
   d) based on

17. Tabernacle
   a) box-like structure in which
      consecrated Hosts are kept
   b) area of the church where the high
      altar stands
   c) area of the church where the
      Baptismal font stands
   d) side altar

18. staff
   a) club
   b) knapsack
   c) fishing pole
   d) walking stick

19. **lad**
   a) boy or young man
   b) boy or young man who is not in school
   c) boy or young man who lives in the country
   d) boy or young man who does not work

20. **youth**
   a) a young man
   b) a young child
   c) a farm worker
   d) a homeless person

A Dishonest Plot

Chapter 18

Perfect Score: 100   Score: _____

1. **dispensing**
   a) selling
   b) displaying
   c) distributing
   d) advertising

2. **articles**
   a) objects
   b) candles
   c) statues
   d) pictures

3. **gravely**
   a) sulkingly
   b) seriously
   c) disappointedly
   d) sadly

4. **unconscious**
   a) unearthly
   b) undisguised
   c) unrecognized
   d) undeveloped

5. **by dint of**
   a) through the power of
   b) instead of
   c) in expectation of
   d) in appreciation of

6. **unlettered**
   a) unwise
   b) mentally slow
   c) not intelligent
   d) unschooled

7. **principal**
   a) middle
   b) most important
   c) most well-known
   d) concluding

8. **disposing of**
   a) giving assistance to
   b) owning, possessing
   c) arranging the affairs of
   d) instructing, educating

9. **scandalous**
   a) shameful, improper
   b) hazardous, dangerous
   c) unbelievable, incredible
   d) embarrassing, ridiculous

10. **contrite**
   a) compassionate
   b) ardent
   c) zealous
   d) repentant

11. **measure**
   a) course of action
   b) good idea
   c) harmful plan
   d) exaggerated problem

12. **affair**
   a) suggestion
   b) problem
   c) plan
   d) matter

VOCABULARY QUIZ WORKBOOK

13. **mockery**
   a) object of fear
   b) object of ridicule
   c) object of disgust
   d) object of disdain

14. **intervene**
   a) put a stop to something
   b) consider something
   c) step in
   d) step down

15. **comic**
   a) puzzling
   b) offensive
   c) humorous
   d) indecent

16. **undignified**
   a) not humble
   b) not acceptable
   c) not respectable
   d) not pleasing

17. **proceedings**
   a) events
   b) disasters
   c) embarrassments
   d) plans

18. **whereupon**
   a) before which
   b) after which
   c) unrelated to which
   d) in spite of which

19. **rebuke**
   a) abuse
   b) restriction
   c) punishment
   d) reprimand

20. **inglorious**
   a) dishonorable
   b) well-deserved
   c) unfortunate
   d) unexpected

The Vicar General
Says "No!"

Chapter 19

Perfect Score: 100

Score: _____

1. **vulgar**
   a) crude, in poor taste
   b) evil, immoral
   c) huge, oversized
   d) ghastly, frightful

2. **scoffed**
   a) griped
   b) insisted
   c) mocked
   d) scolded

3. **jeered**
   a) commented
   b) remarked
   c) laughed
   d) ridiculed

4. **uproarious**
   a) festive and joyous
   b) mean and spiteful
   c) clever and ingenious
   d) noisy and unrestrained

5. **accordingly**
   a) interestingly
   b) consequently
   c) actually
   d) not surprisingly

6. **jests**
   a) curious remarks or acts
   b) violent remarks or acts
   c) joking remarks or acts
   d) jealous remarks or acts

7. **upstart**
   a) person who takes no interest in others
   b) person who rises suddenly to importance
   c) person who takes money from others
   d) person who takes attention away from others

8. **Vicar General**
   a) priest who is in charge in the Bishop's absence
   b) priest who becomes Bishop when the Bishop dies
   c) oldest and wisest priest in the diocese
   d) priest who takes care of all the troublemakers in the diocese

9. **indignities**
   a) offensive, humiliating actions
   b) dishonest, deceitful actions
   c) strange, peculiar actions
   d) destructive, violent actions

10. **hysterical**
    a) absolutely insane
    b) very silly
    c) weeping and sorrowful
    d) uncontrollably emotional

11. **antics**
    a) immoral, sinful behavior
    b) dangerous, unsafe behavior
    c) prideful, boasting behavior
    d) clownish, absurd behavior

12. **summoning**
    a) receiving
    b) announcing to
    c) sending for
    d) sending in

13. **baleful**
    a) foreboding
    b) embarrassed
    c) sudden
    d) annoyed

14. **menacingly**
    a) excitedly
    b) humiliatingly
    c) threateningly
    d) indifferently

15. **upbraid**
    a) defeat thoroughly
    b) scold severely
    c) revolt against
    d) punish justly

16. **astray**
    a) away from that which is popular
    b) away from that which is wrong
    c) away from that which is comfortable
    d) away from that which is right

17. **spellbound**
    a) entranced
    b) quiet
    c) observant
    d) interested

18. **meekly**
    a) zealously
    b) indifferently
    c) quietly
    d) humbly

19. **unjust**
    a) misunderstood
    b) unexpected
    c) unpopular
    d) undeserved

20. **self-possessed**
    a) stubborn
    b) sincere
    c) composed
    d) humble

Chapter 20

Perfect Score: 100   **Score:** _____

1. **vain**
   a) valuable
   b) ignorant
   c) stupid
   d) worthless

2. **assembled**
   a) gathered
   b) traveled
   c) came
   d) worshiped

3. **denounced**
   a) corrected
   b) denied
   c) offended
   d) accused

4. **immeasurably**
   a) somewhat
   b) immensely
   c) unaccountably
   d) effectively

5. **state**
   a) aptitude
   b) condition
   c) attitude
   d) capacity

6. **fruitful**
   a) wonderful
   b) fascinating
   c) profitable
   d) inspiring

7. **spectacle**
   a) public display
   b) public prayer
   c) public announcement
   d) public entertainment

8. **makeshift**
   a) hidden, disguised
   b) broken-down
   c) rickety, flimsy
   d) temporary, substitute

9. **invalids**
   a) caretakers of persons too ill to care
      for themselves
   b) persons suffering from mental illness
   c) persons too ill to care for themselves
   d) persons suffering from the plague

10. **in league with**
    a) learning from
    b) agreeing with
    c) working with
    d) working against

11. **mused**
    a) silently reflected
    b) quietly commented
    c) firmly decided
    d) silently accepted

12. **tersely**
    a) strangely
    b) hurtfully
    c) long-windedly
    d) concisely

13. **promptly**
    a) regretfully
    b) hurriedly
    c) without delay
    d) without regret

14. **resignation**
    a) approval
    b) submission
    c) respect
    d) disobedience

15. gossip
a) lies spread around about someone
b) discussion of publicly known facts
c) stories spread around about someone's private business
d) public announcement of someone's private business

16. borne
a) encouraged
b) lived
c) sacrificed
d) endured

17. worthwhile
a) reasonable, sensible
b) pleasing, enjoyable
c) useful, profitable
d) endurable, bearable

18. startling
a) very surprising
b) very disturbing
c) very troubling
d) very impressive

19. the New World
a) the Far East
b) the Americas
c) the Middle East
d) Africa

20. hardship
a) danger, threat
b) suffering, difficulty
c) challenge, test
d) annoyance, irritation

Walking to Rome

Chapter 21

Text Pages 104-108

Perfect Score: 100

Score: _____

1. circular
a) intended to be returned
b) intended for a few people
c) intended to say goodbye
d) intended for distribution

2. fervent
a) ardent
b) serious
c) excited
d) genuine

3. penning
a) explaining
b) telling
c) writing
d) communicating

4. resolutions
a) great expectations of doing something
b) firm intentions to do something
c) strong desires to do something
d) strict obligations to do something

5. abstain from
a) refrain from
b) decide to do
c) begin to do
d) desist from

6. servile work
a) volunteer work
b) mental work
c) manual labor
d) artistic labor

VOCABULARY QUIZ WORKBOOK

7. **acquaintances**
   a) persons whom one knows
   b) persons whom one likes
   c) persons to whom one is related
   d) persons whom one dislikes

8. **audience**
   a) radio interview
   b) newspaper interview
   c) job interview
   d) formal interview

9. **funds**
   a) assistance
   b) money
   c) authority
   d) preparation

10. **Providence**
    a) God's wisdom
    b) God's justice
    c) God's knowledge
    d) God's care

11. **falter**
    a) increase
    b) waver
    c) decrease
    d) become hidden

12. **stamp out**
    a) protest against
    b) minimize
    c) discourage
    d) eliminate

13. **privileges**
    a) special achievements
    b) special accomplishments
    c) special favors
    d) special acknowledgements

14. **relics**
    a) sacred images of a saint
    b) parts of the body of a saint
    c) holy objects blessed by a saint
    d) devotions established by a saint

15. **yearned**
    a) honestly expected
    b) repeatedly requested
    c) carefully planned
    d) strongly desired

16. **heresy**
    a) immoral behavior
    b) scandal
    c) false belief
    d) drunkenness

17. **in contrast to**
    a) in addition to
    b) as opposed to
    c) similar to
    d) minus

18. **solitary**
    a) unsocial
    b) separate
    c) lone
    d) poor

19. **heretics**
    a) Christians who hold some false
       religious beliefs
    b) Christians who live immoral,
       scandalous lives
    c) persons who worship false gods
    d) persons who deny Christ

20. **custom**
    a) concern
    b) specialty
    c) habit
    d) rule

Audience with the Pope—
And Surprises Back Home

Chapter 22

Text
Pages
109-113

Perfect Score: 100   Score: _____

1. **picturesque**
   a) charming to the eye
   b) of historic importance
   c) of religious importance
   d) having many art galleries

2. **confessor**
   a) priest who runs a parish
   b) priest who hears one's confession
   c) representative of the Pope
   d) assistant to the Pope

3. **vicar**
   a) one who assists someone else
   b) one who takes the place of someone
      else
   c) one who is a student of someone else
   d) one who supports someone else

4. **formal**
   a) stressful, intimidating
   b) normal, usual
   c) strange, weird
   d) official, solemn

5. **Orient**
   a) the North
   b) the South
   c) the East
   d) the West

6. **keen**
   a) pretended
   b) intense
   c) obvious
   d) mild

7. **clad**
   a) adorned
   b) dressed
   c) decorated
   d) disguised

8. **submission**
   a) reluctance
   b) virtue
   c) obedience
   d) shyness

9. **flaunt**
   a) reveal
   b) conceal
   c) show off
   d) encourage

10. **impart**
    a) give, bestow
    b) contribute, donate
    c) lend, loan
    d) present, offer

11. **Papal**
    a) of the Pope
    b) of the Church
    c) of the Saints
    d) of Rome

12. **benediction**
    a) petition
    b) prayer
    c) aid
    d) blessing

13. **invoking**
    a) calling upon
    b) praising
    c) pronouncing
    d) desiring

14. **plenary**
    a) half
    b) partial
    c) immediate
    d) full

15. **indulgence**
    a) removal of the guilt of sin
    b) removal of temporal punishment due for sin
    c) removal of the fear of death
    d) removal of original sin from the soul

16. **doggedly**
    a) determinedly
    b) tiredly
    c) slowly
    d) light-heartedly

17. **postponed**
    a) delayed
    b) cancelled
    c) forgotten
    d) ignored

18. **deceived**
    a) tempted
    b) prevented
    c) fooled
    d) discouraged

19. **hospitality**
    a) good care of the sick
    b) good care of religious
    c) good care of one's family members
    d) good care of guests

20. **evade**
    a) avoid
    b) lie about
    c) complain about
    d) eliminate

Helping to
Make Saints
Discovered!

Chapters 23, 24

Perfect Score: 100

Score: _____

1. **pleading**
    a) requesting
    b) coaxing
    c) debating
    d) begging

2. **were realized**
    a) came true, were made real
    b) came to a halt, stopped
    c) were imagined, were considered
    d) were made known, were publicized

3. **cut to the quick** (figurative meaning)
    a) angered
    b) aggravated
    c) hurt
    d) changed

4. **Pope Clement the Eleventh**
    a) Pope Clement II
    b) Pope Clement IX
    c) Pope Clement XI
    d) Pope Clement XII

5. **lame**
    a) tired or fatigued
    b) shabby or ragged
    c) sickly or ill
    d) crippled or disabled

6. **worn** (referring to a person)
    a) unproductive
    b) undetermined
    c) exhausted
    d) uninterested

7. **shimmering**
   a) glimmering, gleaming
   b) stretching out
   c) appearing
   d) displaying itself

8. **radiant** (literal meaning)
   a) sharp
   b) full
   c) shining
   d) open

9. **Purgatory**
   a) place where souls are tested
   b) place where souls are judged
   c) place where souls are punished and purified
   d) place where souls are punished forever

10. **salvation**
    a) saving
    b) perfecting
    c) calling
    d) sanctifying

----

11. **superior**
    a) person who has authority over another
    b) person who is subject to authority
    c) person who is equal to another in authority
    d) ruler who uses authority oppressively

12. **obscure**
    a) important
    b) old-fashioned
    c) small
    d) little known

13. **identity**
    a) what a person does
    b) interests of a person
    c) who a person is
    d) nickname of a person

14. **tramps**
    a) natives
    b) foreigners
    c) bums
    d) peddlers

15. **oath**
    a) vulgar word
    b) threat
    c) order, command
    d) swear word

16. **to make fast**
    a) to shut loudly or violently
    b) to loosen or open
    c) to lengthen or enlarge
    d) to latch or bolt

17. **attire**
    a) collar
    b) clothing
    c) cassock
    d) disguise

18. **frugal**
    a) scanty
    b) tasteless
    c) not nutritious
    d) not good-tasting

19. **fare**
    a) get along
    b) get going
    c) get up
    d) get set

20. **the elder**
    a) the older of two persons mentioned
    b) the younger of two persons mentioned
    c) the more impressive-looking of two persons mentioned
    d) the more educated of two persons mentioned

The Grumpy Brother
A New Mission

Chapter 25, 26

Text
Pages
124-132

Perfect Score: 100   **Score:** _____

1. had balked at
a) had stubbornly persisted in
b) had objected or refused to
c) had felt unhappy about
d) had forgotten to

2. yield
a) produce
b) display
c) save
d) collect

3. prevailed upon
a) failed to persuade
b) attempted to persuade
c) successfully persuaded
d) persistently coaxed

4. resumed
a) rested from
b) discontinued
c) began
d) began again

5. piously
a) devoutly
b) daily
c) frequently
d) penitentially

6. confided
a) told privately
b) declared firmly
c) announced publicly
d) admitted reluctantly

7. eminent
a) highly intelligent
b) prominent, famous
c) long-time
d) saintly, holy

8. resignedly
a) uninterestedly
b) disgustedly
c) quietly
d) submissively

9. sacristy
a) part of a church around the high altar
b) room where Confessions are usually heard
c) room where sacred vessels and vestments are kept
d) the nave or main body of a church

10. considerable
a) rude, thoughtless
b) deliberate, purposeful
c) fairly large, great
d) unavoidable

11. indicating
a) suggesting
b) assigning
c) ordering
d) pointing out

12. resentful
a) bitter
b) embarrassed
c) frustrated
d) confused

13. uncivil
a) bold
b) discourteous
c) angry
d) deceitful

14. habit
   a) uniform of the priesthood
   b) uniform of a religious order
   c) modest clothing
   d) homespun clothing

---

15. mortify
   a) conceal
   b) subdue
   c) increase
   d) regret

16. sacristan
   a) one who cleans the church
   b) one who cares for the altar and sacristy
   c) one who locks and unlocks the church each day
   d) one who makes the altar linens and vestments

17. culprit
   a) repentant person
   b) guilty person
   c) grumpy person
   d) relative

18. flush
   a) attitude
   b) paleness
   c) blush
   d) smile

19. suppressed
   a) squelched
   b) sarcastic
   c) hearty
   d) light-hearted

20. garrison
   a) military chapel
   b) place where soldiers are stationed
   c) military hospital
   d) battlefield

Ordered to Leave

Chapter 27

Text
Pages
133-138

Perfect Score: 100

Score: _____

1. legend
   a) forgotten story
   b) amazing story
   c) story passed down
   d) newly discovered story

2. reserved
   a) set out
   b) set apart
   c) prophesied
   d) publicized

3. contradicted
   a) opposed
   b) attracted
   c) ignored
   d) observed

4. enterprise
   a) adventure
   b) challenge
   c) obstacle
   d) undertaking

5. issue
a) future
b) foundation
c) satisfaction
d) result

6. flocked
a) traveled despite obstacles
b) walked a long distance
c) went in crowds
d) went two by two

7. ailments
a) fears
b) illnesses
c) problems
d) sorrows

8. bounds
a) obstacles
b) problems
c) decreases
d) limits

9. rallying
a) resisting
b) recovering
c) reassuring
d) remembering

10. maturity
a) adulthood
b) adolescence
c) marriage
d) parenthood

11. passionate
a) sincere, honest
b) devout, pious
c) constant, persistent
d) fervent, intense

12. recompense
a) publicity
b) fame
c) compensation
d) renewal

13. conceal
a) suppress
b) ignore
c) overcome
d) hide

14. mount
a) ascend to
b) descend from
c) approach
d) enter

15. eloquent
a) doctrinally accurate
b) expressive and persuasive
c) holy, sanctified
d) important, essential

16. surpassed
a) equaled
b) suppressed
c) was better than
d) was different from

17. disfavor
a) anger
b) hatred
c) disapproval
d) bitterness

18. bluntly
a) eloquently
b) cruelly
c) subtly
d) frankly

19. immodest
a) protecting purity
b) favoring impurity
c) protecting patience
d) favoring impatience

20. defiance of
a) ignorance of
b) rebellion against
c) defense of
d) disagreement with

A New Companion
and an Old Shrine
Where to Dig?

Chapters 28, 29

Text
Pages
139-148

Perfect Score: 100   Score: _____

1. **oblige**
   a) explain something
   b) exercise authority
   c) perform a service
   d) join a group

2. **account**
   a) defense
   b) condemnation
   c) report
   d) comment

3. **deprived of**
   a) denied
   b) deserted by
   c) longing for
   d) allowed to experience

4. **manual labor**
   a) mental work
   b) physical work
   c) study
   d) works of charity

5. **plausible**
   a) definite
   b) outrageous
   c) hurtful
   d) believable

6. **deserting**
   a) forgetting
   b) ignoring
   c) abandoning
   d) criticizing

7. **pastors**
   a) priests who teach in seminaries
   b) priests who live in monasteries
   c) priests in charge of parishes
   d) priests who assist at parishes

- -

8. **memorial**
   a) something that keeps remembrance alive
   b) something that increases virtue
   c) something that adds beauty
   d) something that provides a benefit

9. **promising**
   a) perfect in every way
   b) very much appreciated
   c) providing good expectations
   d) having been sought for a long time

10. **site**
    a) time
    b) mountaintop
    c) location
    d) arrangement

11. **retired**
    a) returned
    b) re-entered
    c) fled
    d) withdrew

12. **resume**
   a) conclude
   b) begin again
   c) begin
   d) analyze

13. **excavation**
   a) place where planning has occurred
   b) place where digging has occurred
   c) place where building has occurred
   d) place where planting has occurred

14. **nestling**
   a) sitting
   b) cooing
   c) snuggling
   d) lying

15. **vigil**
   a) a period of thought and planning
   b) a period of staying awake and praying at night
   c) a period of time spent praying in church
   d) a period of time spent sleeping in church

16. **a host of**
   a) a bundle of
   b) a multitude of
   c) a small group of
   d) a series of

17. **summit**
   a) hill, mountain
   b) outdoor shrine
   c) scene, landscape
   d) hilltop, mountaintop

18. **bearing**
   a) supporting
   b) symbolizing
   c) reflecting
   d) connecting

19. **representations**
   a) paintings
   b) statues
   c) drawings
   d) images

20. **duplicate**
   a) display
   b) exhibit
   c) copy
   d) dramatize

The Calvary
at Pontchâteau

Chapter 30

Perfect Score: 100   **Score:** _____

1. **arduous**
   a) difficult, strenuous
   b) time-consuming
   c) dull, boring
   d) devout, pious

2. **buoyed up**
   a) weighed down
   b) changed
   c) supported
   d) joined together

3. **strain**
   a) pain
   b) illness
   c) injury
   d) stress

4. **base**
   a) back
   b) middle
   c) summit
   d) foundation

5. yoke
    a) pair of animals joined by a bar
    b) line of animals
    c) trailer for transporting animals
    d) group of animals

6. recruited
    a) volunteered
    b) enlisted
    c) ordered
    d) sought

7. folk
    a) people
    b) strangers
    c) adults
    d) workers

8. were possessed of
    a) deserved
    b) desired
    c) had
    d) donated

9. means
    a) fame
    b) integrity
    c) dignity
    d) wealth

10. descend
    a) come down
    b) get out
    c) move away
    d) exit

11. recruit
    a) new member
    b) new supervisor
    c) visitor
    d) observer

12. noble
    a) high-ranking
    b) rich
    c) pious
    d) fashionable

13. labors
    a) interests
    b) virtue
    c) intentions
    d) work

14. toil
    a) anxiety and worry
    b) high hopes
    c) hard work
    d) good intentions

15. dotting
    a) ornamenting, adorning
    b) completely covering
    c) scattered here and there on
    d) hiding from view

16. landscaped
    a) paved with concrete
    b) paved with pebbles
    c) ornamented with lawn furniture
    d) ornamented with plantings

17. righteous
    a) obvious
    b) evident
    c) stubborn
    d) justified

18. solemn
    a) celebrated with a banquet
    b) publicized in advance
    c) marked by formal religious rites
    d) lasting a long time

19. exaltation
    a) holiness
    b) glorification
    c) commemoration
    d) procession

20. vows
    a) promises
    b) ceremonies
    c) petitions
    d) virtues

Perfect Score: 100   Score: _____

1. **massing**
   a) lining up
   b) wandering about freely
   c) forming a circle
   d) forming a large group

2. **drawn**
   a) carried
   b) pulled
   c) followed
   d) led

3. **contents**
   a) that which is contained in
      something
   b) that which is excluded from
      something
   c) that which is added to something
   d) that which is deleted from
      something

4. **scanned**
   a) read aloud
   b) glanced over
   c) stared at
   d) studied intently

5. **peculiar**
   a) frightened
   b) odd
   c) serious
   d) puzzled

6. **pilgrims**
   a) persons on a pleasure trip
   b) persons who spend much time
      in prayer
   c) persons on a religious journey
   d) persons who have very strong faith

7. **protested**
   a) informed
   b) grumbled
   c) pointed out
   d) objected

8. **induce**
   a) prepare
   b) satisfy
   c) force
   d) persuade

9. **dumbfounded**
   a) shocked, speechless
   b) angry, enraged
   c) disobedient, rebellious
   d) wretched, miserable

10. **camouflaged**
    a) military
    b) barricaded
    c) disguised
    d) fortified

11. **fortress**
    a) hideout
    b) stronghold
    c) prison camp
    d) lookout post

12. **customary**
    a) humble
    b) usual
    c) necessary
    d) kindly

13. **withdrew from**
    a) lost interest in
    b) maintained position in
    c) moved back from
    d) observed silence regarding

14. **retirement**
    a) participation in action
    b) retreat from action
    c) reparation and penance
    d) banishment, exile

15. celebrated
   a) very successful
   b) very busy
   c) pious, devout
   d) famous

16. lawful
   a) spiritual
   b) rightful
   c) virtuous
   d) respected

17. layman
   a) unordained person
   b) hermit
   c) servant
   d) disorderly person

18. hence
   a) therefore
   b) heretofore
   c) from now
   d) from then

19. Friars Preachers
   a) Franciscans
   b) Carmelites
   c) Dominicans
   d) Benedictines

20. forlornly
   a) unconcernedly
   b) miserably
   c) anxiously
   d) trustingly

Mission to
the Calvinists

Chapter 32

Text
Pages
159-162

Perfect Score: 100   Score: _____

1. cultivating
   a) preserving
   b) nurturing
   c) renewing
   d) spreading

2. aims
   a) goals
   b) rules
   c) rewards
   d) duties

3. at sea (figurative meaning)
   a) depressed, pessimistic
   b) disgusted, irritated
   c) fearful, worried
   d) lost, bewildered

4. derived
   a) expressed
   b) enjoyed
   c) dedicated
   d) received

5. indication
   a) application
   b) evidence
   c) expectation
   d) understanding

6. exhibited
   a) had
   b) practiced
   c) showed
   d) taught

7. laden
   a) moved
   b) loaded
   c) floated
   d) rowed

8. provisions
   a) supplies
   b) weapons
   c) passengers
   d) refugees

9. **expedition**
   a) journey made by a large group
      of persons
   b) journey made for rescue purposes
   c) journey made for a specific purpose
   d) journey involving danger to life
      and limb

10. **fleet**
    a) group of men working together
    b) group of vehicles or boats operating
       together
    c) group of vehicles or boats lined up
       in a row
    d) group of vehicles or boats arranged
       in a circle

11. **capsizing**
    a) splintering
    b) sinking
    c) turning around
    d) turning over

12. **cargo**
    a) goods being transported
    b) goods being stored
    c) food and medical supplies
    d) goods packed in boxes

13. **venture**
    a) risky undertaking
    b) famous undertaking
    c) educational undertaking
    d) merciful undertaking

14. **acclaimed**
    a) reluctantly admitted to be
    b) rewarded as
    c) appreciated as
    d) enthusiastically proclaimed

15. **relent**
    a) resist
    b) yield
    c) respond
    d) stand firm

16. **leveled**
    a) made flat
    b) made rough
    c) made unusable
    d) made dangerous

17. **a hundredfold**
    a) added to a hundred
    b) subtracted from a hundred
    c) multiplied by a hundred
    d) divided by a hundred

18. **wholly**
    a) entirely
    b) somewhat
    c) definitely
    d) obviously

19. **jubilant**
    a) filled with quiet satisfaction
    b) joyous, exultant
    c) filled with great hope
    d) motivated by firm determination

20. **doctrine**
    a) teaching
    b) law
    c) custom
    d) promise

Verdict of the
Three Canons

Chapter 33

Text
Pages
163-169

Perfect Score: 100

Score: _____

1. **misdeeds**
   a) sufferings
   b) mistakes
   c) problems
   d) sins

2. **confessional**
   a) place for receiving the Sacrament of Confirmation
   b) place for receiving the Sacrament of Penance
   c) place for receiving the Sacrament of Holy Orders
   d) place for receiving the Sacrament of Extreme Unction (Last Anointing)

3. **waylay**
   a) await and then attack
   b) follow and then attack
   c) attack in a group
   d) shout at

4. **plots**
   a) public plans
   b) secret plans
   c) public disagreements
   d) secret disagreements

5. **learned** (used as an adjective)
   a) very intelligent
   b) very knowledgeable
   c) very prudent
   d) famous

6. **canon**
   a) priest who lives in a monastery
   b) priest assigned to a cathedral
   c) priest who is pastor of a parish
   d) priest who is sent to the foreign missions

7. **inconspicuously**
   a) unnoticeably
   b) unmistakeably
   c) unofficially
   d) inoffensively

8. **render**
   a) understand, decipher
   b) begin, initiate
   c) present, turn in
   d) advise, counsel

9. **respectively**
   a) in that manner
   b) in that order
   c) respectfully
   d) responsibly

10. **madman**
    a) lunatic
    b) swindler
    c) rascal
    d) villain

11. **fuming**
    a) discouragement, disappointment
    b) malice, ill will
    c) agitation, irritation
    d) silent sulking

12. **pride**
    a) excessive, improper self-esteem
    b) lack of proper self-esteem
    c) excessive, improper esteem for private property
    d) lack of proper esteem for private property

13. **barring**
   a) with
   b) in addition to
   c) by means of
   d) except for

14. **advises**
   a) describes
   b) counsels
   c) explains
   d) tells

15. **favored**
   a) looked down on
   b) looked up to with great respect
   c) showed special kindness toward
   d) took pity on

16. **substance**
   a) goodness, virtue
   b) essence, meaning
   c) offering, gift
   d) help, assistance

17. **consulted**
   a) stared at
   b) pretended to look at
   c) looked for
   d) referred to

18. **produced**
   a) examined, analyzed
   b) prepared, made ready
   c) brought forward
   d) protected from harm

19. **evident**
   a) secret
   b) obvious
   c) devoted
   d) unrestrained

20. **relish**
   a) pleasure
   b) sincerity
   c) understanding
   d) reverence

Pirates! | # Chapter 34 | Text Pages 170-174

Perfect Score: 100   Score: _____

1. **grateful**
   a) happy
   b) gracious
   c) thankful
   d) relieved

2. **foiling**
   a) predicting
   b) ensuring the success of
   c) foreseeing
   d) preventing the success of

3. **band**
   a) group
   b) conspiracy
   c) pair
   d) trio

4. **cutthroats**
   a) criminals
   b) thieves
   c) vandals
   d) murderers

5. **assassin**
   a) murderer, especially of a prominent person
   b) murderer, especially of a homeless person
   c) murderer, especially in France
   d) murderer, especially one using a sword

6. wrought
   a) placed
   b) worked
   c) preserved
   d) ensured

7. sheathe
   a) take a sword or knife out of its covering
   b) pick up a sword or knife
   c) put a sword or knife into its covering
   d) wield a sword or knife

8. infested with
   a) overrun with
   b) famous for
   c) frequented by
   d) favored by

9. martyrs
   a) persons who are killed for Christ
   b) persons who suffer for Christ
   c) persons who profess the Faith
   d) persons who are killed

10. mortally
   a) unfortunately
   b) morally
   c) irrationally
   d) deathly

11. port
   a) capital city of a nation
   b) place where slaves are bought and sold
   c) place where ships load and unload
   d) place where pirates attack ships

12. tonic
   a) something that educates
   b) something that invigorates
   c) something that inspires
   d) something that uplifts

13. reluctant
   a) resolved
   b) indifferent
   c) eager
   d) hesitant

14. voyage
   a) dangerous journey
   b) journey by water
   c) religious journey
   d) pleasant journey

15. ominous
   a) dark
   b) ugly
   c) threatening
   d) large

16. despair
   a) exhaustion
   b) panic
   c) terror, great fear
   d) loss of hope

17. cowered
   a) crouched in fear
   b) took cover
   c) shut one's eyes in fear
   d) surrendered

18. prow
   a) front of a boat
   b) left side of a boat
   c) right side of a boat
   d) rear of a boat

19. craft
   a) boat, especially for sailing
   b) boat, especially for fishing
   c) boat, especially of large size
   d) boat, especially of small size

20. vessels
   a) warships
   b) large ships
   c) pirate ships
   d) stolen ships

Hopes for
the Future

Chapter 35

Text
Pages
175-180

Perfect Score: 100   Score: _____

1. **billowing**
   a) signalling or motioning
   b) flapping in the wind
   c) swelling or puffing out
   d) wavering or shifting

2. **spyglass**
   a) small telescope
   b) eyeglasses
   c) pair of binoculars
   d) bifocals

3. (cannons) **trained**
   a) shot
   b) placed
   c) triggered
   d) pointed

4. **strains**
   a) hymns
   b) melodies
   c) verses
   d) words

5. *Magnificat*
   a) canticle (sacred song) of the Blessed
      Virgin Mary
   b) canticle of Simeon
   c) canticle of Our Lord
   d) canticle of St. Joseph

6. **qualm**
   a) confident feeling
   b) misgiving
   c) objection
   d) desire, wish

7. **mainland**
   a) islands surrounding a country
   b) capital of a country
   c) chief body of land of a country
   d) islands that make up a country

8. **occupation**
   a) pace of life
   b) environment
   c) habitual activity
   d) status, rank

9. **at leisure**
   a) often, frequently
   b) at intervals
   c) in solitude
   d) unhurriedly

10. **idly**
    a) desperately, urgently
    b) shrewdly, watchfully
    c) inactively, lazily
    d) stupidly, idiotically

11. **sow** (literal meaning)
    a) plant
    b) cultivate
    c) irrigate
    d) harvest

12. **premonition**
    a) feeling of forewarning
    b) feeling of regret
    c) feeling of bewilderment
    d) feeling of boredom

13. **manuscript**
    a) unpublished writing
    b) writing on a religious topic
    c) famous writing
    d) unfinished writing

14. **Rule** (of a religious order)
    a) the Ten Commandments
    b) a single regulation that members
       of a religious order must follow
    c) set of regulations that members
       of a religious order must follow
    d) set of suggestions that members of
       a religious order may follow

15. candidates
   a) potential members
   b) actual members
   c) previous members
   d) members

16. seminary
   a) school in which men learn how to be priests
   b) school in which men learn how to be religious brothers
   c) school in which men learn how to be missionaries
   d) school in which men learn how to teach

17. Ordination
   a) the conferring of Confirmation
   b) the conferring of Holy Orders
   c) ceremony of making vows in a religious order
   d) ceremony of entering a seminary

18. banished
   a) conquered
   b) destroyed
   c) avoided
   d) expelled

19. direction
   a) commendation
   b) guidance
   c) analysis
   d) inquiry

20. accounts
   a) attempts
   b) reports
   c) possibilities
   d) directions

Surprise for
Sister Mary Louise
A Broken Promise

Chapters 36, 37

Text
Pages
181-191

Perfect Score: 100

Score: _____

1. thriving
   a) adapting
   b) changing
   c) prospering
   d) surviving

2. efficient
   a) devoted, faithful
   b) punctual, prompt
   c) thoughtful, careful
   d) effective, capable

3. outcasts
   a) persons who are rejected
   b) persons who are depressed
   c) persons who are diseased
   d) persons who are dependent

4. benefactors
   a) donors
   b) followers
   c) companions
   d) acquaintances

5. veritable
   a) unfortunate, upsetting
   b) real, true
   c) crazy, insane
   d) persistent, enduring

6. lively
   a) worldly and superficial
   b) stylish and sophisticated
   c) energetic and active
   d) rude and abrupt

7. **endear oneself**
   a) make oneself loved
   b) make oneself respected
   c) make oneself accepted
   d) make oneself understood

8. **seaport**
   a) capital
   b) harbor
   c) fishery
   d) seacoast

9. **catechism**
   a) basic religious truths
   b) reading, writing and arithmetic
   c) advanced theology
   d) spiritual direction

10. **dispel**
    a) cover up
    b) drive away
    c) destroy
    d) heal

11. **inmates**
    a) persons who live near each other
    b) members of a group or organization
    c) persons employed by an institution
    d) persons living in an institution

12. **downcast**
    a) frustrated
    b) dejected
    c) disturbed
    d) distracted

13. **instrument**
    a) missionary
    b) inmate
    c) priest
    d) tool

14. **forth**
    a) onward
    b) promptly
    c) between third and fifth
    d) determinedly

15. **pulpit**
    a) piece of furniture used for kneeling
    b) piece of furniture used for dining
    c) piece of furniture used in meditating
    d) piece of furniture used in preaching

16. **well-nigh**
    a) overly
    b) extremely
    c) completely
    d) nearly

17. **progressed**
    a) concluded, closed
    b) began, started
    c) continued, proceeded
    d) intensified

18. **credentials**
    a) equipment and supplies
    b) official documents
    c) travel plans
    d) reference books

19. **pagans**
    a) those who claim there is no God
    b) those who have abandoned the
       True Religion
    c) those who do not believe in the
       true God
    d) those who live in foreign lands

20. **frantically**
    a) in a perplexed manner
    b) in a frenzied manner
    c) somewhat uneasily
    d) disgustedly, with annoyance

The Bargain
The Last Words
of a Saint

Chapters 38, 39

Text
Pages
192-201

Perfect Score: 100   **Score: _____**

1. advanced
   a) paid before work is done
   b) paid after work is done
   c) paid on time
   d) paid late

2. bound
   a) motivated
   b) desiring
   c) intending
   d) obligated

3. reimburse
   a) repay, refund
   b) apologize to
   c) lend money to
   d) borrow money from

4. zest
   a) great effort
   b) dignity
   c) hearty enjoyment
   d) a strong sense of responsibility

5. frail
   a) weak, fragile
   b) odd, strange
   c) sick, diseased
   d) determined, strong-willed

6. convulsed
   a) knocked down
   b) shaken violently
   c) afflicted with pain
   d) suffocated

7. utterly
   a) almost
   b) absolutely
   c) probably
   d) very

8. virtues
   a) acts of moral goodness
   b) habits of moral goodness
   c) desires to be morally good
   d) knowledge of moral goodness

9. glistened
   a) glared
   b) glowed
   c) sparkled
   d) brightened

10. numb
   a) incapable of feeling emotion
   b) incapable of understanding
   c) incapable of moving
   d) incapable of showing emotion

11. tuberculosis
   a) a disease that affects primarily the
      heart
   b) a disease that affects primarily the
      pancreas
   c) a disease that affects primarily the
      joints
   d) a disease that affects primarily the
      lungs

12. asthma
   a) a cardiac disorder
   b) a gastric disorder
   c) a skeletal disorder
   d) a respiratory disorder

13. **racking**
   a) wrenching, straining
   b) wretched, miserable
   c) persistent, continuous
   d) annoying, bothersome

14. **consternation**
   a) irritation, annoyance
   b) dismay and confusion
   c) welcome surprise
   d) overwhelming gratitude

15. **the Last Sacraments**
   a) Penance, Holy Communion and Holy Viaticum
   b) Penance, Extreme Unction and Last Anointing
   c) Penance, Plenary Indulgence and Papal Blessing
   d) Penance, Extreme Unction and Holy Viaticum

16. **throngs**
   a) crowds
   b) sorrowful people
   c) orphans
   d) elderly women

17. **indifferent**
   a) perfect
   b) mediocre
   c) unknown
   d) unlikely

18. **schemed**
   a) made successful plans
   b) made unsuccessful plans
   c) made underhanded plans
   d) lied

19. **shunned**
   a) deliberately rejected
   b) deliberately misrepresented
   c) deliberately avoided
   d) deliberately attacked

20. **murmured**
   a) said reassuringly
   b) said confidently
   c) said softly
   d) whispered

Continuing the Great Work	**Epilogue**	Text Pages 202-211

Perfect Score: 100   Score: _____

1. **beset by**
   a) conquered by
   b) concerned with
   c) occupied with
   d) troubled by

2. **seclusion**
   a) isolation
   b) desperation
   c) hiding
   d) rebellion

3. **Easter Duty**
   a) attending Mass on Easter Sunday
   b) receiving Communion during the Easter season
   c) attending Mass on Holy Thursday
   d) attending Church services during Holy Week

4. **prospering**
   a) thriving
   b) continuing
   c) perpetuating itself
   d) being publicized

5. defray
   a) cancel
   b) pay
   c) invest in
   d) loan

6. the Revolution
   a) the Russian Revolution of 1789
   b) the World Revolution of 1789
   c) the Roman Revolution of 1789
   d) the French Revolution of 1789

7. pillaged
   a) tortured and murdered
   b) set on fire
   c) looted and destroyed
   d) captured

8. pioneer
   a) best, most efficient
   b) earliest, original
   c) most experienced
   d) most enthusiastic

9. all-embracing
   a) strong
   b) holy
   c) wise
   d) total

10. diabolical
   a) raging
   b) devilish
   c) sharp
   d) hideous

11. coffer
   a) chest that holds valuables
   b) chest that holds a corpse
   c) underground storage room
   d) attic

12. conjectured
   a) announced
   b) publicized
   c) decided
   d) guessed

13. presided at
   a) conducted the ceremonies at
   b) made a public appearance at
   c) participated in the ceremonies at
   d) took photographs at

14. beatification
   a) proclamation by the Pope that a deceased person is Venerable
   b) proclamation by the Pope that a deceased person is Blessed
   c) proclamation by the Pope that a deceased person is a Saint
   d) proclamation by the Pope that a deceased person is a martyr

15. successor
   a) person who has been elected to serve in a position
   b) person who shares a position with another
   c) person who holds a position after another does
   d) person who holds a position before another does

16. Apostolic Benediction
   a) perpetual remembrance
   b) partial indulgence
   c) plenary indulgence
   d) papal blessing

17. the Belgian Congo
   a) country in Europe
   b) country in Asia
   c) country in Africa
   d) country in Central America

18. adversary
   a) opponent, enemy
   b) defender, protector
   c) one who exposes
   d) one who explains

19. guise
    a) external appearance
    b) excuse
    c) failure
    d) foundation, basis

20. salutary
    a) strong, powerful
    b) beneficial, healthful
    c) widespread, far-reaching
    d) unique, unequaled

LISTS OF
VOCABULARY WORDS

VOCABULARY WORDS

Word	Chapter	Word	Chapter	Word	Chapter	Word	Chapter	Word	Chapter
recitation	15	sacrilege	1	startled	3	sympathizing with	5	vigil	10
recourse to, had	14	sanctuary	14	steadfastly	9			vigorously	8
recreation	7	scant	3	stern	8	theology	9	vision	13
refrained from	13	scheme	9	stock	6	throng	10	vow	14
refuge	4	scoffed	4	strain	7	tolled	12		
regarded	13	scruples	8	strayed, have	2	tone	13	wagged, (tongues)	5
remains	15	secular	14	stricken with	13	trebles	7	wanly	14
reparation	1	seminary	9	stupendous	11	tribute	15	wasted	12
requiem	12	sensible	8	sublime	1	tuberculosis	11	well-founded	15
resembled	5	shafts	10	submission	1	twilight	7	well-nigh	14
resolutely	4	shimmering	2	subscription	15			wistfully	4
revelation	5	slyly	3	succeeded	13	unleashed	11		
reverenced	14	soberly	13	sufficient	8	unwittingly	15		
reverently	5	solemn	7	summons	6				
revolving	10	spectacle	10	supernatural	9	vain, in	6		
rigorous	11	speculated	12	superstitious	11	venerated	15		
rival	6	spellbound	10	supplication	10	vent	13		
		spin	11	surmounted by	1	ventured	2		
		splendid	12	surpassed	13	victim	11		
sacrifice	1	stamped out	15	suspended	1, 12				

VOCABULARY WORDS

Book Two	THE CURÉ OF ARS	Workbook Pages 27-57

Word	Chapter	Word	Chapter	Word	Chapter	Word	Chapter	Word	Chapter
abandoned to, be	5	calamity	13	deserters	4	flocked	12	intercede	20
abating	20	candidate for	2	designs	5	foretaste	11	intercession	13
abreast of, keep	5	canon	6	desolate	16	forlorn	5	invalids	12
abruptly	2	canonized	11	despatched	15	forsaken	15	irregular	6
absolution	7	capacity	5	detachment, (army)	4	foster	19	
absorbed in	2	Catacombs	14	detestable	16	foundation	17	Jerusalem	20
accompanied	1	catechist	19	devout	14	francs	17	justifiable	2
acknowledged	1	channels	1	dialect	7	frank	7	justified	8
administered	7	charge	19	dilapidated	7	frantically	4	
admittance	11	choicest	20	din	10	frontier	4	keen	5
ado, without more	6	christening	8	dint of, by	13	frantically		
afflicted	17	Church Militant	13	diocese	9	funds	9	landscape	15
age-old	15	circulate	12	dire	8			lapsed	15
ailment	12	clambered	5	dirge	18	gnawing	9	lashed	20
ambitions	3	clamoring	13	disclose	15	goodly	3	Last Rites	20
amidst (amid)	18	climax	10	disgrace	4	graces	3	latter	9
ancestral	8	coarse	8	dishonored	11	gravely	6	launched	16
anew	10	coaxing	1	dismay	4	grimly	15	laymen	11
Angelus	18	cobbler	18	dismissed	16	grudge	16	laywomen	17
anonymous	9	commenced, had	6	dispensation	6	guild	8	learned	6
archdiocese	9	commit oneself	14	distinction	5			likewise	18
assail	13	comparatively	17	distinguished	19	handyman	5	litany	16
assistant	7	compensated (for)	14	distressing	15	haste	14	longingly	2
assume	10	conceal	16	down-hearted	2	hazard	8	lukewarm	2
attain	19	conduct	20	dowry	2	headstrong	11	lurch	10
attentively	16	conducted	2	due	10	heaving	10	
avail oneself of	13	confided	14			heed	14	major seminary	7
		confraternity	8	earnestly	3	heedless of	20	makeshift	1
bade farewell	15	conscious	4	ebbing	20	hermit	16	malice	9
beck and call, at everyone's	15	consecrated	13	embraced	15	hitherto	9	manifested	17
benefactor	4	consolation	1	emphatic	6	hoisted	4	manufacturer	7
bereft of	10	conspicuous	8	enlightenment	6	Holy Sacrifice, the	20	marred	5
besieged with	16	conviction	7	entitled to, be	5	hubbub	10	massing	18
bestowed	12	crisis	2	enveloped	11	huskiest	10	mastering	7
bewilderment	12	cultivate	12	ermine	17			matchwood	9
bitterness	18	curate	18	evident	11	idlers	12	materialized	12
boarders	9			exertion	14	immense	10	merit	3
borne	9	deferred	5	exile	1	impelled	19	merits (noun)	11
Breviary	14	defray	17	expense	2	imperial	19	mildly	11
brink	14	dense	4	Extreme Unction	20	imprudent	3	ministered to	3
briskly	13	departure	5			impulse	7	miser	17
burdens	13	deputation	9	faltered	3	inaugurate	17	mission	17
		descend upon	10	feeble	20	inclined, was	2	missionary	3
		deserted	15	ferry	9	incredulously	19	mortifications	3
				fervent	11	indignant	8	mortified	5
						infirm	13	mournful	20
						instrument	16	

VOCABULARY WORDS

Word	Chapter	Word	Chapter	Word	Chapter	Word	Chapter	Word	Chapter
abandonment	11	captive	10	enrolled	5	indebted to	11	obstinate	5
accompany	2	caress	3	estate	3	indifferent	10	onslaughts	15
accordance		cast	15	Eternal City,		indignant	4	oratory	10
with, in	13	catacombs	7	the	7	Indochina	13	orderly	10
acquire	12	cell	8	Eternal Life	15	infinite	12	Orient, the	13
adorned	9	chanced upon	11	eve	10	infirmary	14		
advanced	3	channel	12	ever-present	15	iniquity	14	pagans	6
affairs	6	chanting	8	excavations	7	inserted	15	pale	1
affectionate	2	charge	9	exclusive	8	institution	3	paralysis	9
afflicted	1	chastity	9	excursions	3	intention	2	parlor	4
agony	8	cherished	6	exiles	3	intercession	11	parted	1
air	2	circular	14	existence	14	intervals	2	penetration	12
alas	1	climax	7					Pentecost	6
alter	2	cloister	1	fatigue	13	labor	10	permanently	2
ambitious	14	Clothing Day	9	feast	6	liberty	5	persisted	6
amiable	14	confided	13	fervent	1	literary	12	pertaining to	12
amid	5	confiding	15	flattered	3	longed	6	picturesque	7
amused	2	confine	8	fortified	15	lot	14	pilgrimage	6
angling	3	confirmed	9	fortitude	5			plagued	4
anxiety	14	consecrated to	1	fragments	7	malady	10	pondered	9
apparently	5	consecration to	5	fresco	10	manifest	15	possess	11
arose	6	consent	6			mankind	12	postulant	8
assembled	10	consolation	13	gaping	7	martyrdom	7	preceding	5
assisted at		content	8	garb	8	marveled at	1	prescribed	14
(Mass)	8	contented	1	gay	13	masterpiece	12	presently	1
atone for	12	contrary,		glazed (eyes)	11	Matins	10	presume	7
attainment, of	12	(on the)	1	glory	8	meditation	5	pretexts	14
avail	4	conversion	6	godmother	1	Memorare	5	prevailed	8
awaited	2	convey	13	grating	3	merit	12	prey to, fell	13
		counsel	5	gratitude	6	mild	9	prioress	6
banish	5	cross	2	gravely	13	mite	1	proceeded	7
barricade	7	curt	7	grieving	2	model	4	procession	1
bass	3	customary	3	grounds	11	moderate	8	profoundly	11
bewilderment	9					mortify	13	progress	11
bitterly	3	deceit	2	harvest	13	mount	11	promptly	4
blasphemed	6	delegate	8	hastened	15	multitude	15	pronounced	5
blessed, the	3	departure	4	heartily	1	murmured	3	prospect	7
Blessed (Bl.)	13	despair	15	heed	10			prospering	1
bliss	11	discern	14	heedless	7	namely	12	prostrate	10
boarding		Divine Office	8	heights	2	noble	14	published	15
school	2	due	3	henceforth	9	noted	6	purchased	3
borne	13	duly	10	hermit	4	novena	4	Purgatory	3
brethren	13			humanity	1	novice	9		
		earnestly	2	humiliation	12			quick	8
calamity	4	ecstasies	10			objection	11		
canon	6	elect, (the)	14	immense	12	observances	13	radiant	4
capacity	14	employed	2	imploring	4	obstacle	16	raiment	9

VOCABULARY WORDS

Word	Chapter	Word	Chapter	Word	Chapter	Word	Chapter	Word	Chapter
abruptly	3	conviction	7	grieved	7	Orient, the	3	stormed	4
absorbed	7	courteous	1					suspended	6
affection	3	crucifix	3	hardships	5	peculiar	2		
aim	2	crude	5	hasten	7	persecution	4	tapestries	3
ambassador	1	customary	6	hearth	3	persevere	5	temples	3
anxiously	2			heresy	2	prioress	7	theology	2
ardent	5	decked	4	humiliations	5	prolonged	6	thoroughly	7
assembled	5	deftly	1			prominent	1	threshold	5
astonished	3	departure	7	immense	7	prostrated	6	timid	5
awkwardly	3	destination	1	inquired	5			transported	2
		deter	7	inscription	4	quarters	1	tunic	5
bid	1	devoutly	3	intercede	6	quivering	3	twined	3
binding	4	dismay	3						
boastfully	3	doctrine	4	lamely	1	rapture	6	unaccustomed	2
breathtaking	7	Donna	1	lilting	3	rash	1	unhindered	6
		dwelling	3	literary	6	recess	1	uttered	7
carefree	6					refectory	5		
caressed	3	ecstasy	6	martyr	4	render	1	Vespers	4
catacombs	4	elaborate	3	marveled	7	reproachful	2	vigil	6
ceased	4	enlightened,		merchant	1	resolutely	1	vigorously	2
century	2	has	6	migrated	4	restraining	7		
charge	4			motley	1	revelry	2	weariness	7
clad	2	failing	1	mourn	6	reverently	6	whereupon	2
clamor	1	falter	5	murmured	2	rheumatism	4	wistful	3
clamored for	7	fervently	1			Rhineland	6	withdrew	7
clever	4	festive	1	nobility	2				
cloister	5	flares	2	novice	5	sanctuary	7	yielded	5
cloistered	4	flocked	7	novice mistress	7	save	4		
commotion	2	fostered	4			scanned	2		
Communion of Saints	4	founder	2	obscured	6	scapular	5		
		frail	1	onlookers	7	scarce	5		
Confiteor	6	friars	4			sentiments	6		
consecrated (Host)	6			Order of Preachers, the	4	shrewdly	5		
		glistening	5			slumber	2		
consoled	6	gravely	5			solemn	3		

VOCABULARY WORDS

VOCABULARY WORDS—THE MIRACULOUS MEDAL

VOCABULARY WORDS

VOCABULARY QUIZ WORKBOOK

ANSWER KEY

ANSWER KEY

Book One	THE CHILDREN OF FATIMA	Workbook Pages 3-25

Chapter 1

1) d		11) b	
2) a		12) c	
3) b		13) c	
4) d		14) a	
5) b		15) a	
6) b		16) c	
7) d		17) c	
8) b		18) c	
9) a		19) a	
10) b		20) d	

Chapter 2

1) c		11) b	
2) a		12) b	
3) c		13) d	
4) a		14) c	
5) d		15) a	
6) b		16) b	
7) a		17) c	
8) d		18) c	
9) b		19) d	
10) a		20) a	

Chapter 3

1) c		11) b	
2) b		12) d	
3) b		13) c	
4) b		14) a	
5) d		15) c	
6) c		16) b	
7) b		17) b	
8) a		18) d	
9) d		19) b	
10) a		20) c	

Chapter 4

1) b		11) b	
2) b		12) c	
3) b		13) a	
4) d		14) c	
5) c		15) a	
6) a		16) d	
7) d		17) b	
8) c		18) a	
9) a		19) d	
10) c		20) c	

Chapter 5

1) a		11) d	
2) a		12) b	
3) c		13) a	
4) d		14) a	
5) c		15) d	
6) b		16) b	
7) c		17) c	
8) d		18) b	
9) b		19) b	
10) a		20) c	

Chapter 6

1) a		11) a	
2) b		12) a	
3) c		13) b	
4) a		14) d	
5) d		15) d	
6) d		16) c	
7) c		17) a	
8) a		18) d	
9) d		19) b	
10) b		20) b	

Chapter 7

1) d		11) c	
2) b		12) b	
3) a		13) a	
4) a		14) a	
5) c		15) b	
6) b		16) d	
7) d		17) b	
8) c		18) b	
9) a		19) c	
10) c		20) d	

Chapter 8

1) a		11) a	
2) c		12) b	
3) b		13) b	
4) d		14) c	
5) a		15) c	
6) b		16) c	
7) a		17) b	
8) b		18) d	
9) a		19) b	
10) d		20) c	

Chapter 9

1) d		11) a	
2) c		12) b	
3) c		13) c	
4) b		14) a	
5) b		15) b	
6) a		16) a	
7) a		17) d	
8) b		18) a	
9) b		19) d	
10) c		20) d	

Chapter 10

1) a		11) a	
2) b		12) c	
3) c		13) d	
4) a		14) c	
5) b		15) d	
6) a		16) c	
7) b		17) b	
8) b		18) d	
9) b		19) b	
10) b		20) d	

Chapter 11

1) a		11) c	
2) d		12) a	
3) d		13) a	
4) b		14) a	
5) c		15) b	
6) b		16) c	
7) a		17) a	
8) b		18) c	
9) d		19) c	
10) b		20) d	

Chapter 12

1) a		11) d	
2) d		12) d	
3) b		13) d	
4) c		14) c	
5) c		15) b	
6) a		16) d	
7) d		17) a	
8) a		18) a	
9) a		19) a	
10) b		20) c	

Chapter 13

1) a		11) c	
2) c		12) b	
3) a		13) a	
4) c		14) d	
5) b		15) d	
6) c		16) a	
7) c		17) d	
8) c		18) a	
9) d		19) b	
10) a		20) c	

Chapter 14

1) a		11) a	
2) c		12) c	
3) c		13) b	
4) d		14) b	
5) c		15) d	
6) b		16) a	
7) b		17) c	
8) d		18) d	
9) d		19) b	
10) a		20) a	

Chapter 15

1) d		11) c	
2) a		12) a	
3) b		13) d	
4) b		14) b	
5) a		15) d	
6) b		16) d	
7) c		17) b	
8) b		18) d	
9) c		19) a	
10) b		20) d	

ANSWER KEY

Chapter 1

1) c	11) b
2) b	12) a
3) a	13) c
4) b	14) a
5) d	15) c
6) b	16) a
7) d	17) d
8) b	18) b
9) c	19) a
10) d	20) c

Chapter 2

1) d	11) b
2) d	12) b
3) d	13) a
4) c	14) a
5) a	15) b
6) d	16) c
7) a	17) c
8) c	18) b
9) b	19) d
10) b	20) a

Chapter 3

1) c	11) a
2) d	12) a
3) a	13) a
4) d	14) c
5) c	15) d
6) a	16) b
7) b	17) b
8) c	18) b
9) b	19) a
10) c	20) b

Chapter 4

1) b	11) d
2) c	12) c
3) a	13) a
4) d	14) d
5) a	15) a
6) b	16) b
7) c	17) c
8) b	18) c
9) b	19) d
10) a	20) a

Chapter 5

1) c	11) a
2) a	12) c
3) c	13) b
4) a	14) b
5) d	15) b
6) c	16) a
7) a	17) c
8) b	18) c
9) b	19) d
10) d	20) c

Chapter 6

1) a	11) b
2) b	12) d
3) b	13) a
4) a	14) a
5) c	15) d
6) a	16) b
7) c	17) b
8) a	18) d
9) a	19) a
10) b	20) c

Chapter 7

1) b	11) c
2) b	12) d
3) c	13) a
4) c	14) c
5) a	15) c
6) b	16) d
7) a	17) a
8) b	18) d
9) a	19) d
10) b	20) b

Chapter 8

1) c	11) b
2) a	12) a
3) a	13) c
4) d	14) b
5) a	15) a
6) d	16) c
7) b	17) d
8) c	18) d
9) b	19) a
10) b	20) a

Chapter 9

1) d	11) c
2) a	12) a
3) a	13) c
4) b	14) a
5) b	15) b
6) c	16) d
7) a	17) a
8) a	18) d
9) a	19) a
10) b	20) b

Chapter 10

1) c	11) a
2) d	12) b
3) d	13) d
4) a	14) a
5) c	15) b
6) b	16) c
7) b	17) c
8) d	18) a
9) d	19) d
10) c	20) c

Chapter 11

1) d	11) a
2) a	12) b
3) c	13) a
4) a	14) c
5) a	15) b
6) c	16) d
7) b	17) a
8) a	18) b
9) a	19) c
10) d	20) b

Chapter 12

1) c	11) b
2) b	12) c
3) a	13) a
4) c	14) a
5) a	15) d
6) d	16) b
7) b	17) c
8) c	18) c
9) b	19) a
10) d	20) d

Chapter 13

1) c	11) b
2) d	12) c
3) a	13) b
4) a	14) c
5) b	15) d
6) c	16) b
7) b	17) c
8) d	18) b
9) c	19) c
10) a	20) a

Chapter 14

1) a	11) d
2) a	12) c
3) c	13) a
4) d	14) b
5) c	15) a
6) d	16) c
7) a	17) b
8) b	18) b
9) c	19) d
10) b	20) b

Chapter 15

1) c	11) a
2) a	12) a
3) c	13) b
4) b	14) c
5) d	15) d
6) a	16) b
7) b	17) a
8) c	18) d
9) d	19) b
10) c	20) a

Chapter 16

1) a	11) d
2) d	12) b
3) b	13) c
4) b	14) d
5) c	15) c
6) d	16) b
7) a	17) b
8) c	18) a
9) d	19) d
10) a	20) b

Chapter 17

1) a   11) a
2) d   12) b
3) d   13) b
4) a   14) d
5) b   15) c
6) c   16) a
7) c   17) b
8) b   18) c
9) c   19) d
10) a   20) c

Chapter 18

1) c   11) b
2) d   12) a
3) d   13) a
4) a   14) c
5) c   15) d
6) b   16) a
7) d   17) d
8) c   18) a
9) a   19) b
10) c   20) c

Chapter 19

1) c   11) b
2) d   12) c
3) a   13) c
4) b   14) a
5) b   15) d
6) c   16) d
7) d   17) a
8) c   18) d
9) b   19) b
10) a   20) c

Chapter 20

1) a   11) d
2) d   12) b
3) b   13) d
4) a   14) b
5) d   15) a
6) c   16) c
7) c   17) a
8) b   18) d
9) d   19) d
10) c   20) c

ANSWER KEY

Chapter 1

1) a	11) b
2) b	12) c
3) d	13) d
4) b	14) a
5) d	15) d
6) b	16) b
7) c	17) a
8) a	18) c
9) a	19) d
10) b	20) b

Chapter 2

1) a	11) d
2) b	12) c
3) d	13) a
4) c	14) c
5) a	15) c
6) b	16) d
7) b	17) b
8) d	18) b
9) a	19) a
10) c	20) b

Chapter 3

1) d	11) b
2) a	12) a
3) b	13) b
4) d	14) b
5) c	15) b
6) a	16) c
7) c	17) b
8) c	18) b
9) d	19) a
10) a	20) a

Chapter 4

1) c	11) b
2) b	12) a
3) a	13) a
4) b	14) d
5) c	15) b
6) c	16) c
7) d	17) b
8) a	18) a
9) d	19) d
10) a	20) a

Chapter 5

1) b	11) b
2) d	12) d
3) a	13) d
4) a	14) a
5) c	15) d
6) a	16) c
7) b	17) d
8) c	18) d
9) a	19) a
10) c	20) b

Chapter 6

1) a	11) d
2) b	12) d
3) d	13) c
4) b	14) b
5) c	15) d
6) c	16) c
7) b	17) a
8) b	18) c
9) c	19) b
10) a	20) c

Chapter 7

1) d	11) b
2) a	12) d
3) a	13) c
4) b	14) b
5) c	15) b
6) a	16) c
7) b	17) c
8) b	18) b
9) d	19) d
10) c	20) b

Chapter 8

1) b	11) a
2) b	12) b
3) c	13) a
4) d	14) d
5) c	15) a
6) a	16) d
7) d	17) c
8) b	18) b
9) c	19) b
10) c	20) c

Chapter 9

1) c	11) b
2) b	12) c
3) d	13) c
4) b	14) c
5) c	15) d
6) a	16) c
7) a	17) d
8) b	18) a
9) d	19) d
10) b	20) d

Chapter 10

1) a	11) b
2) c	12) d
3) c	13) b
4) b	14) b
5) b	15) c
6) a	16) d
7) a	17) b
8) d	18) d
9) d	19) d
10) c	20) a

Chapter 11

1) a	11) a
2) c	12) a
3) b	13) b
4) c	14) c
5) d	15) a
6) a	16) b
7) b	17) d
8) d	18) b
9) c	19) a
10) b	20) c

Chapter 12

1) b	11) c
2) b	12) c
3) a	13) d
4) c	14) a
5) c	15) b
6) d	16) c
7) a	17) a
8) b	18) d
9) c	19) b
10) b	20) b

Chapter 13

1) a	11) c
2) a	12) d
3) c	13) d
4) d	14) c
5) a	15) b
6) d	16) a
7) c	17) c
8) a	18) a
9) d	19) a
10) d	20) b

Chapter 14

1) c	11) b
2) a	12) d
3) a	13) b
4) b	14) c
5) c	15) d
6) d	16) c
7) a	17) c
8) d	18) b
9) a	19) b
10) c	20) a

Chapter 15

1) c	11) b
2) b	12) c
3) b	13) d
4) c	14) a
5) d	15) a
6) b	16) b
7) b	17) b
8) a	18) b
9) c	19) a
10) a	20) c

ANSWER KEY

Book Four	PATRON SAINT OF FIRST COMMUNICANTS	Workbook Pages 83-93

Chapter 1

1) b	11) c		
2) b	12) a		
3) a	13) c		
4) c	14) a		
5) c	15) c		
6) d	16) b		
7) d	17) d		
8) a	18) a		
9) a	19) c		
10) a	20) b		

Chapter 2

1) a	11) a
2) b	12) a
3) c	13) c
4) d	14) a
5) b	15) b
6) a	16) d
7) b	17) c
8) b	18) a
9) d	19) b
10) a	20) c

Chapter 3

1) b	11) c
2) b	12) c
3) d	13) d
4) c	14) a
5) b	15) b
6) c	16) c
7) a	17) a
8) a	18) b
9) c	19) d
10) c	20) d

Chapter 4

1) a	11) b
2) b	12) c
3) d	13) b
4) d	14) c
5) b	15) a
6) b	16) a
7) a	17) b
8) d	18) a
9) a	19) c
10) d	20) b

Chapter 5

1) b	11) b
2) d	12) b
3) c	13) b
4) d	14) a
5) b	15) c
6) a	16) b
7) c	17) b
8) a	18) d
9) a	19) c
10) a	20) b

Chapter 6

1) b	11) b
2) c	12) b
3) c	13) a
4) c	14) d
5) d	15) c
6) a	16) b
7) a	17) b
8) c	18) a
9) b	19) c
10) d	20) a

Chapter 7

1) c	11) a
2) b	12) d
3) b	13) c
4) d	14) c
5) b	15) b
6) d	16) b
7) c	17) a
8) a	18) d
9) c	19) c
10) d	20) d

ANSWER KEY

Chapter 1

1) d		11) a	
2) c		12) d	
3) b		13) a	
4) c		14) c	
5) b		15) d	
6) a		16) b	
7) d		17) c	
8) b		18) a	
9) b		19) a	
10) a		20) d	

Chapters 2, 3

1) a		11) c	
2) c		12) b	
3) d		13) d	
4) b		14) b	
5) c		15) d	
6) c		16) d	
7) d		17) d	
8) b		18) b	
9) a		19) c	
10) b		20) d	

Chapters 4, 5

1) b		11) c	
2) a		12) b	
3) a		13) d	
4) b		14) a	
5) d		15) b	
6) a		16) b	
7) d		17) b	
8) c		18) a	
9) a		19) c	
10) a		20) b	

Chapters 6, 7

1) b		11) d	
2) a		12) a	
3) d		13) b	
4) b		14) a	
5) c		15) d	
6) d		16) c	
7) d		17) c	
8) b		18) b	
9) b		19) b	
10) b		20) d	

Chapters 8, 9

1) c		11) a	
2) a		12) c	
3) a		13) c	
4) d		14) d	
5) c		15) a	
6) c		16) b	
7) a		17) c	
8) b		18) b	
9) d		19) d	
10) d		20) d	

Chapters 10, 11, 12

1) b		11) d	
2) c		12) c	
3) c		13) b	
4) b		14) d	
5) d		15) a	
6) a		16) a	
7) d		17) c	
8) c		18) b	
9) a		19) b	
10) a		20) c	

Chapters 13, 14

1) d		11) c	
2) a		12) b	
3) d		13) c	
4) d		14) a	
5) b		15) c	
6) b		16) d	
7) a		17) b	
8) c		18) b	
9) b		19) a	
10) d		20) d	

Chapter 15

1) a		11) a	
2) d		12) d	
3) c		13) b	
4) b		14) c	
5) a		15) a	
6) c		16) a	
7) b		17) c	
8) d		18) d	
9) a		19) a	
10) c		20) c	

Chapter 16

1) d		11) b	
2) b		12) d	
3) a		13) b	
4) c		14) c	
5) b		15) b	
6) d		16) a	
7) d		17) c	
8) a		18) b	
9) c		19) b	
10) a		20) b	

Chapter 17

1) d		11) b	
2) c		12) b	
3) a		13) d	
4) b		14) c	
5) b		15) b	
6) d		16) a	
7) b		17) c	
8) a		18) c	
9) a		19) d	
10) c		20) a	

Chapters 18, 19

1) c		11) b	
2) c		12) a	
3) b		13) c	
4) c		14) d	
5) a		15) a	
6) a		16) b	
7) d		17) b	
8) c		18) a	
9) c		19) d	
10) d		20) c	

Chapters 20, 21

1) c		11) c	
2) b		12) c	
3) d		13) b	
4) d		14) b	
5) a		15) d	
6) c		16) c	
7) a		17) a	
8) d		18) b	
9) d		19) c	
10) a		20) a	

ANSWER KEY

Chapter 1

1) b		11) d	
2) c		12) b	
3) a		13) a	
4) b		14) c	
5) d		15) d	
6) a		16) b	
7) c		17) b	
8) c		18) d	
9) d		19) d	
10) a		20) a	

Chapter 2

1) d		11) a	
2) a		12) c	
3) b		13) b	
4) b		14) b	
5) c		15) a	
6) a		16) b	
7) d		17) d	
8) d		18) b	
9) b		19) c	
10) b		20) a	

Chapter 3

1) a		11) c	
2) c		12) d	
3) c		13) a	
4) b		14) b	
5) d		15) b	
6) b		16) d	
7) b		17) c	
8) d		18) c	
9) c		19) b	
10) b		20) d	

Chapters 4, 5

1) c		11) b	
2) d		12) a	
3) d		13) d	
4) c		14) a	
5) a		15) a	
6) c		16) c	
7) b		17) d	
8) d		18) b	
9) d		19) c	
10) c		20) d	

Chapters 6, 7

1) b		11) b	
2) c		12) a	
3) a		13) a	
4) b		14) b	
5) d		15) b	
6) d		16) a	
7) b		17) d	
8) b		18) b	
9) a		19) c	
10) c		20) c	

Chapter 8

1) b		11) a	
2) c		12) b	
3) a		13) b	
4) c		14) b	
5) d		15) d	
6) d		16) a	
7) a		17) b	
8) c		18) d	
9) d		19) b	
10) b		20) a	

Chapter 9

1) c		11) d	
2) a		12) c	
3) a		13) b	
4) d		14) d	
5) b		15) d	
6) c		16) b	
7) b		17) a	
8) d		18) d	
9) d		19) d	
10) c		20) c	

Chapter 10

1) d		11) c	
2) a		12) b	
3) d		13) d	
4) b		14) b	
5) b		15) c	
6) c		16) a	
7) a		17) c	
8) b		18) a	
9) d		19) a	
10) a		20) b	

Chapter 11

1) d		11) d	
2) a		12) b	
3) d		13) c	
4) b		14) b	
5) b		15) b	
6) a		16) c	
7) c		17) a	
8) c		18) c	
9) d		19) d	
10) a		20) c	

Chapter 12

1) d		11) d	
2) a		12) c	
3) b		13) b	
4) d		14) a	
5) c		15) a	
6) d		16) d	
7) d		17) b	
8) b		18) c	
9) b		19) b	
10) a		20) b	

Chapter 13

1) b		11) a	
2) c		12) a	
3) a		13) c	
4) a		14) b	
5) d		15) c	
6) a		16) d	
7) c		17) d	
8) d		18) a	
9) c		19) b	
10) b		20) b	

Chapter 14

1) b		11) b	
2) a		12) d	
3) d		13) a	
4) a		14) d	
5) c		15) c	
6) b		16) b	
7) b		17) a	
8) d		18) d	
9) d		19) b	
10) a		20) c	

Chapter 15

1) d		11) d	
2) c		12) c	
3) b		13) c	
4) a		14) a	
5) c		15) b	
6) c		16) b	
7) a		17) c	
8) d		18) d	
9) b		19) c	
10) b		20) a	

Chapters 16, 17

1) a		11) d	
2) d		12) c	
3) c		13) c	
4) c		14) a	
5) a		15) c	
6) c		16) b	
7) a		17) a	
8) d		18) d	
9) b		19) a	
10) a		20) a	

Chapter 18

1) c		11) a	
2) a		12) d	
3) b		13) b	
4) c		14) c	
5) a		15) c	
6) d		16) c	
7) b		17) a	
8) c		18) b	
9) a		19) d	
10) d		20) a	

Chapter 19

1) a		11) d	
2) c		12) c	
3) d		13) a	
4) d		14) c	
5) b		15) b	
6) c		16) d	
7) b		17) a	
8) a		18) d	
9) a		19) d	
10) d		20) c	

Chapter 20

1) d	11) a		
2) a	12) d		
3) d	13) c		
4) b	14) b		
5) b	15) c		
6) c	16) d		
7) a	17) c		
8) d	18) a		
9) c	19) b		
10) c	20) b		

Chapter 21

1) d	11) b
2) a	12) d
3) c	13) c
4) b	14) b
5) a	15) d
6) c	16) c
7) a	17) b
8) d	18) c
9) b	19) a
10) d	20) c

Chapter 22

1) a	11) a
2) b	12) d
3) b	13) a
4) d	14) d
5) c	15) b
6) b	16) a
7) b	17) a
8) c	18) c
9) c	19) d
10) a	20) a

Chapters 23, 24

1) d	11) a
2) a	12) d
3) c	13) c
4) c	14) c
5) d	15) d
6) c	16) d
7) a	17) b
8) c	18) a
9) c	19) a
10) a	20) a

Chapters 25, 26

1) b	11) d
2) a	12) a
3) c	13) b
4) d	14) b
5) a	15) b
6) a	16) b
7) b	17) b
8) d	18) c
9) c	19) a
10) c	20) b

Chapter 27

1) c	11) d
2) b	12) c
3) a	13) d
4) d	14) a
5) d	15) b
6) c	16) c
7) b	17) c
8) d	18) d
9) b	19) b
10) a	20) b

Chapters 28, 29

1) c	11) d
2) c	12) b
3) a	13) b
4) b	14) c
5) d	15) b
6) c	16) b
7) c	17) d
8) a	18) a
9) c	19) d
10) c	20) c

Chapter 30

1) a	11) a
2) c	12) a
3) d	13) d
4) d	14) c
5) a	15) c
6) b	16) d
7) a	17) d
8) c	18) c
9) d	19) b
10) a	20) a

Chapter 31

1) d	11) b
2) b	12) b
3) a	13) c
4) b	14) b
5) b	15) d
6) c	16) b
7) d	17) a
8) d	18) c
9) a	19) c
10) c	20) b

Chapter 32

1) b	11) d
2) a	12) a
3) d	13) a
4) d	14) d
5) b	15) b
6) c	16) a
7) b	17) c
8) a	18) a
9) c	19) b
10) b	20) a

Chapter 33

1) d	11) c
2) b	12) a
3) a	13) d
4) b	14) b
5) b	15) c
6) b	16) b
7) a	17) d
8) c	18) c
9) b	19) b
10) a	20) a

Chapter 34

1) c	11) c
2) d	12) b
3) a	13) d
4) d	14) b
5) a	15) c
6) b	16) d
7) c	17) a
8) a	18) a
9) a	19) d
10) d	20) b

Chapter 35

1) c	11) a
2) a	12) a
3) d	13) a
4) b	14) c
5) a	15) a
6) b	16) a
7) c	17) b
8) c	18) d
9) d	19) b
10) c	20) b

Chapters 36, 37

1) c	11) d
2) d	12) b
3) a	13) d
4) a	14) a
5) b	15) d
6) c	16) d
7) a	17) c
8) b	18) b
9) a	19) c
10) b	20) b

Chapters 38, 39

1) a	11) d
2) d	12) d
3) a	13) a
4) c	14) b
5) a	15) d
6) b	16) a
7) b	17) b
8) b	18) c
9) c	19) c
10) a	20) c

Chapter Epilogue

1) d	11) a
2) a	12) d
3) b	13) a
4) a	14) b
5) b	15) c
6) d	16) d
7) c	17) c
8) b	18) a
9) d	19) a
10) b	20) b

6 Great Catholic Books for Children

. . . and for all young people ages 10 to 100!!

1137 THE CHILDREN OF FATIMA—And Our Lady's Message to the World. 162 pp. PB. 15 Illus. Impr. The wonderful story of Our Lady's appearances to little Jacinta, Francisco and Lucia at Fatima in 1917. **11.00**

1138 THE CURÉ OF ARS—The Story of St. John Vianney, Patron Saint of Parish Priests. 211 pp. PB. 38 Illus. Impr. The many adventures that met young St. John Vianney when he set out to become a priest. . . .**13.00**

1139 THE LITTLE FLOWER—The Story of St. Therese of the Child Jesus. 167 pp. PB. 24 Illus. Impr. Tells what happened when little Therese decided to become a saint. **11.00**

1140 PATRON SAINT OF FIRST COMMUNICANTS—The Story of Blessed Imelda Lambertini. 85 pp. PB. 14 Illus. Impr. Tells of the wonderful miracle God worked to answer little Imelda's prayer. **8.00**

1141 THE MIRACULOUS MEDAL—The Story of Our Lady's Appearances to St. Catherine Labouré. 107 pp. PB. 21 Illus. Impr. The beautiful story of what happened when young Sister Catherine saw Our Lady. **9.00**

1142 ST. LOUIS DE MONTFORT—The Story of Our Lady's Slave. 211 pp. PB. 20 Illus. Impr. The remarkable story of the priest who went around helping people become "slaves" of Jesus through Mary. **13.00**

1136 ALL 6 BOOKS ABOVE (Reg. 65.00) . . . . **THE SET: 52.00**

1841 VOCABULARY QUIZ WORKBOOK **21.00**
1919 SET: VOCABULARY QUIZ WORKBOOK
     & 6 BOOKS above (Reg. 86.00). **68.00**

6 <u>More</u> Great Catholic Books for Children

1200 SAINT THOMAS AQUINAS—The Story of "The Dumb Ox." 81 pp. PB. 16 Illus. Impr. The remarkable story of how St. Thomas, called in school "The Dumb Ox," became the greatest Catholic teacher ever. . . . **8.00**

1201 SAINT CATHERINE OF SIENA—The Story of the Girl Who Saw Saints in the Sky. 65 pp. PB. 13 Illus. The amazing life of the most famous Catherine in the history of the Church. **7.00**

1202 SAINT HYACINTH OF POLAND—The Story of The Apostle of the North. 189 pp. PB. 16 Illus. Impr. Shows how the holy Catholic Faith came to Poland, Lithuania, Prussia, Scandinavia and Russia. **13.00**

1203 SAINT MARTIN DE PORRES—The Story of The Little Doctor of Lima, Peru. 122 pp. PB. 16 Illus. Impr. The incredible life and miracles of this black boy who became a great saint. **10.00**

1204 SAINT ROSE OF LIMA—The Story of The First Canonized Saint of the Americas. 132 pp. PB. 13 Illus. Impr. The remarkable life of the little Rose of South America. **10.00**

1205 PAULINE JARICOT—Foundress of the Living Rosary and The Society for the Propagation of the Faith. 244 pp. PB. 21 Illus. Impr. The story of a rich young girl and her many spiritual adventures. . **15.00**

1206 ALL 6 BOOKS ABOVE (Reg. 63.00) . . . . **THE SET: 50.00**

Prices subject to change.

8 More Great Catholic Books for Children

... and for all young people ages 10 to 100!!

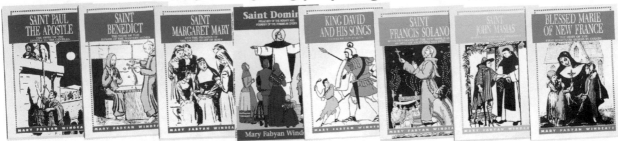

1230 SAINT PAUL THE APOSTLE—The Story of the Apostle to the Gentiles. 231 pp. PB. 23 Illus. Impr. The many adventures that met St. Paul in the early Catholic Church. **15.00**

1231 SAINT BENEDICT—The Story of the Father of the Western Monks. 158 pp. PB. 19 Illus. Impr. The life and great miracles of the man who planted monastic life in Europe. **11.00**

1232 SAINT MARGARET MARY—And the Promises of the Sacred Heart of Jesus. 224 pp. PB. 21 Illus. Impr. The wonderful story of remarkable gifts from Heaven. Includes St. Claude de la Colombière. **14.00**

1233 SAINT DOMINIC—Preacher of the Rosary and Founder of the Dominican Order. 156 pp. PB. 19 Illus. Impr. The miracles, trials and travels of one of the Church's most famous saints. **11.00**

1234 KING DAVID AND HIS SONGS—A Story of the Psalms. 138 pp. PB. 23 Illus. Impr. The story of the shepherd boy who became a warrior, a hero, a fugitive, a king, and more. **11.00**

1235 SAINT FRANCIS SOLANO—Wonder-Worker of the New World and Apostle of Argentina and Peru. 205 pp. PB. 19 Illus. Impr. The story of St. Francis' remarkable deeds in Spain and South America. **14.00**

1236 SAINT JOHN MASIAS—Marvelous Dominican Gatekeeper of Lima, Peru. 156 pp. PB. 14 Illus. Impr. The humble brother who fought the devil and freed a million souls from Purgatory. **11.00**

1237 BLESSED MARIE OF NEW FRANCE—The Story of the First Missionary Sisters in Canada. 152 pp. PB. 18 Illus. Impr. The story of a wife, mother and nun—and her many adventures in pioneer Canada. **11.00**

1238 ALL 8 BOOKS ABOVE (Reg. 98.00) . . . . **THE SET: 78.00**

Prices subject to change.

Get the Complete Set!! ...

SET OF ALL 20 TITLES
by Mary Fabyan Windeatt

(Individually priced—226.00   Reg. set prices—180.00)

1256 THE SET OF ALL 20 . . . . **Only 160.00**

U.S. & CAN. POST./HDLG.: $1-$10, add $3; $10.01-$25, add $5; $25.01-$50, add $6; $50.01-$75, add $7; $75.01-$150, add $8; $150.01 or more, add $10.

Based on the traditional Catholic Bible (Douay-Rheims) ...

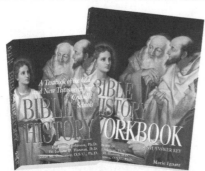

No. 1819. SET OF BOTH BOOKS.
Reg. 45.00
Set Price 35.00

BIBLE HISTORY—A Textbook of the Old and New Testaments for Catholic Schools. By Fr. George Johnson, Ph.D., Fr. Jerome Hannan, D.D. and Sister M. Dominica, O.S.U., PhD. 558 Pp. PB. 1931. Impr. 165 Illus. 23 Maps. Index. We give this book 5 stars! ISBN-6928.
No. 1776   **24.00**

BIBLE HISTORY WORKBOOK with Answer Key. Marie Ignatz. To accompany the above. 179 Pp. PB. 8 1/2 x 11. Over 2,400 Answer Blanks, with 50-100 Completion and Matching Exercises for each chapter! Nice large type. Fun to use! Great! ISBN-7037.
No. 1792   **21.00**

Provides a tremendous Catholic foundation in Scripture!

Wonderful Catholic History Texts . . .

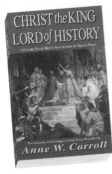

CHRIST THE KING—LORD OF HISTORY. Anne W. Carroll. 474 Pp. PB. Index. A fast-paced, enjoyable, highly readable, fascinating, interesting Catholic world history for **high school and adult reading.** Covers largely Western world history from a Catholic viewpoint. Just flows and flows, with one interesting episode after another of our glorious history; one captivating historical personage after another. Unabashedly proud of our Catholic heritage. This book makes the Church the central figure of *all* history, which it is. Don't miss it! (ISBN-5034).

No. 1228 **24.00**

CHRIST THE KING, LORD OF HISTORY—WORKBOOK AND STUDY GUIDE, With Answer Key. Belinda T. Mooney. 192 Pp. 8 1/2 x11. PB. Over 50 Questions for each of the 30 Chapters. To write right in the book. Excellent! Fun to use! (ISBN-6731). **No. 1754 21.00**

SET: CHRIST THE KING, LORD OF HISTORY and WORKBOOK.

No. 1766 (Reg. 45.00) **36.00**

CHRIST AND THE AMERICAS. Anne W. Carroll. 440 Pp. PB. Index. Great Catholic **high school history.** Gives the role of the Catholic Church in American history. Starts with the earliest explorers and concludes with the 1990s. Covers American history in a fast-paced, thorough, interesting manner. Scores of amazing insights. Makes history really come alive. Great for students; stimulating and informative reading for adults also. U.S. and Central and South American history beautifully woven together. Each era gets its own in-depth coverage. Gives a great sense of American history. We give it 5 stars! (ISBN-5948).

No. 1387 **24.00**

CHRIST AND THE AMERICAS—WORKBOOK AND STUDY GUIDE, With Answer Key. Belinda T. Mooney. **No. 1884** **21.00**

SET: CHRIST AND THE AMERICAS and WORKBOOK.

No. 1921 (Reg. 45.00) **36.00**

THE OLD WORLD AND AMERICA. Most Rev. Philip J. Furlong. 384 Pp. PB. Impr. 200 illus. A famous **5th-8th grade** world history. Introduces the student to hundreds of important persons, events, places, dates and concepts. 37 chapters, with Study Questions and Activities. From Creation and the Flood to the Greeks, Romans, the Church, Middle Ages, Renaissance, Protestant Revolt, etc., up to early exploration of the New World. Manifests great respect for our Western heritage, Our Lord and the Catholic Church. Illustrations, maps, index, pronunciation key. Perfect background for *CHRIST THE KING—LORD OF HISTORY.* (ISBN-2027).

No. 1002 **21.00**

OUR PIONEERS AND PATRIOTS. Most Rev. Philip J. Furlong. 505 Pp. PB. Impr. 235 Illus. & maps. Index. A famous **5th-8th grade** American history textbook written in 1940 with Catholic faith and patriotic love of country. 55 Chapters, with Study Questions & Activities. Teaches *a lot* in a simple manner: From early exploration and settlement through 20th-century developments. By the end of this book the student will be familiar with the famous people, places, dates and events in U.S. history and have a tremendous store of knowledge to build on when pursuing greater understanding at a more advanced level. Perfect background for *CHRIST AND THE AMERICAS.* Great! (ISBN-5921).

No. 1396 **24.00**

OLD WORLD AND AMERICA —ANSWER KEY. 96 Pp. PB. (ISBN-6200).

No. 1550 **10.00**

SET: OLD WORLD AND AMERICA and ANSWER KEY.
No. 1854 (Reg. 31.00) **27.00**

OUR PIONEERS AND PATRIOTS—ANSWER KEY. 94 Pp. PB. (ISBN-6065).

No. 1529 **10.00**

SET: OUR PIONEERS AND PATRIOTS and ANSWER KEY.
No. 1855 (Reg. 34.00) **29.00**

Extremely valuable resources that will save hours for the busy teacher or homeschooling parent. Will also enable the 5th-8th grade student to work his way independently through each text. Clear, easy to use, well laid out, with page numbers for easy reference. Any potential difficulties are noted. Make using the text a pleasure.

At your Bookdealer or direct from the Publisher.

TAN BOOKS AND PUBLISHERS, INC. • P.O. BOX 424 • ROCKFORD, ILLINOIS 61105
TOLL FREE: 1-800-437-5876 Tel: 815-226-7777 www.tanbooks.com

Prices subject to change.

Like a Catholic *Tom Sawyer!!* . . .

Fr. Francis J. Finn, S.J.
1859-1928
(Each book includes
a 2-page "About the Author")

These books are among Fr. Finn's 27 Catholic novels for young people. Resembling a Catholic version of Charles Dickens' stories, or even of *Tom Sawyer*, these books were read by hundreds of thousands of young people in the late 19th and early-to-mid 20th centuries. Their quaint turn-of-the-century language is part of the charm of these stories and of Fr. Finn's own brand of humor. After young readers (or hearers) have gotten into his style, they find it hilarious! (Grades 5-8—and up!)

CLAUDE LIGHTFOOT—Or How the Problem Was Solved. 263 pp. PB. The story opens upon CLAUDE LIGHTFOOT, a reckless 12-year-old boy who constantly acts first and thinks later. After being injured in a clash with some bullies, Claude is obliged to miss his First Communion. In the course of the story, Fr. Finn manages to cover a host of topics, including smoking, drinking, the devil, Confession, Holy Communion, retaining one's Baptismal innocence, the 9 First Fridays, the priesthood, mothers and sisters, truthfulness, lying, courage, effeminacy, atheism, sacrilege, baseball, Americanism (true and false), Latin, virtue, honor, leadership, etc.

As the story unfolds, Claude's adventures will take a most unexpected turn, as Fr. Finn once again presents the reader with a great picture of the All-American Catholic boy! ISBN-7126. **No. 1801** 9.00

THAT FOOTBALL GAME—And What Came of It. 262 pp. PB. This book features Claude Lightfoot, Willie Hardy and many other characters from *Claude Lightfoot*. Again, Fr. Finn covers a multitude of Catholic topics, giving a ringing defense of the game of football and presenting a great picture of the All-American Catholic boy! ISBN-7134. **No. 1802** 9.00

ETHELRED PRESTON—Or the Adventures of a Newcomer. 237 pp. PB. In this book, the new kid certainly livens things up at Henryton boarding academy! Again, Fr. Finn covers all kinds of Catholic topics and presents a great picture of the All-American Catholic boy! ISBN-7142. **No. 1803** 9.00

1804 Set of Claude Lightfoot, That Football Game *and* Ethelred Preston (Reg. 27.00) **21.00**

Plus, *"Fr. Finn's Famous Three"!!* . . .

TOM PLAYFAIR—Or Making a Start. 255 pp. PB. Tom's adventures at a Jesuit boarding academy! ISBN-6707. **No. 1755** 9.00

PERCY WYNN—Or Making a Boy of Him. 248 pp. PB. A boy who has grown up with his 10 sisters meets Tom Playfair and his friends! ISBN-6715. **No. 1756** 9.00

HARRY DEE—Or Working It Out. 284 pp. PB. Harry's adventures with Tom P. and Percy W. Also called *The Mystery of Tower Hill Mansion!* ISBN-6723. **No. 1757** 9.00

1758 Set of Tom Playfair, Percy Wynn *and* Harry Dee (Reg. 27.00) **21.00**

1920 Set of All 6 Fr. Finn Books (Reg. 54.00) **39.00**

At your Bookdealer or direct from the Publisher.

TAN BOOKS AND PUBLISHERS, INC. • **P.O. BOX 424** • **ROCKFORD, ILLINOIS 61105**
TOLL FREE: 1-800-437-5876 **Tel: 815-226-7777** **www.tanbooks.com**
Prices subject to change.